Gomidas Institute Studies Series

Talaat Pasha's Report on the Armenian Genocide, 1917

by Ara Sarafian

Gomidas Institute
London

This work was originally published as a special study by the Gomidas Institute in 2011. It has now been expanded with some minor changes and the addition of eight new color maps and illustrations.

ISBN 978-1-909382-72-5   03 04 05

Gomidas Institute
42 Blythe Rd.
London W14 0HA
United Kingdom
Email: *info@gomidas.org*
Web: *www.gomidas.org*

CONTENTS

MAPS AND ILLUSTRATIONS

Introduction

Talaat stated that "they had already disposed of three quarters of them [Armenians], that there were none left in Bitlis, Van, Erzeroum, and that the hatred was so intense now that they have to finish it. . . . He said they would take care of the Armenians at Zor and elsewhere but they did not want them in Anatolia. I told him three times that they were making a serious mistake and would regret it. He said, 'We know we have made mistakes, but we never regret.'"

—Diaries of Ambassador Henry Morgenthau[1]

Supervising the Destruction of Armenians

Throughout 1915–16, Talaat Pasha, the Ottoman Minister of Interior, supervised the destruction of Armenians in the Ottoman Empire. Masking this process as a security measure, he ordered the general deportation of Armenians and monitored the break-up of communities with the murder of hundreds of thousands of people through privations and outright killings, the forced conversions and absorption of Armenians into Muslim households, the systematic confiscation of properties, and the dispersion of survivors across the empire. Talaat received progress reports from different provinces and, at the end of 1916, ordered a general assessment of his work. On 24 August 1916, he sent a cipher telegram to 34 provinces (vilayets and mutasarrifliks) asking for detailed information about the presence of Armenians in different parts of the empire.[2] His circular was simple and to the point: he wanted to know the number and whereabouts of Armenians in each province, as well as how many of them were "natives" (*yerli*), or "outsiders" (*yabancı*), at each location. Six months later, on 11 February 1917, he sent another cipher telegram, this time to 23 provinces, calling for a headcount of Armenians.[3] Once more, he asked for the number of "native" and "outsider" Armenians in each region.

Talaat's Report on the Destruction of Ottoman Armenians

In 2008 the Turkish journalist and historian Murat Bardakçı published a report from Talaat's private papers concerning Armenians in the Ottoman Empire.[4] This report was obviously commissioned by Talaat Pasha and was obtained from his widow shortly before her death in 1982.[5] It was based on a study showing the distribution of Armenians in

Ottoman provinces and was prepared with great care. Although it bore no date, title, or formal introduction, the document started with summary calculations of the number of Ottoman Armenians in 1914 and 1917. These calculations gave a breakdown of the number of Armenians in each province in 1914, as well as the number of Armenians from each province counted in different parts of the Ottoman Empire in 1917.[6] A note pointed out that the raw figures were undercounts and estimated the prewar Ottoman Armenian population (excluding Protestant Armenians) at approximately 1,500,000 people, with 350,000 to 400,000 Armenians of all denominations remaining in 23 provinces in 1917.[7] According to Talaat's adjusted figures, around 1,150,000 Ottoman Armenians (or 77 percent) had disappeared between 1914 and 1917.[8]

Turkish Archives and the Deportation of Armenians

In recent years, the Turkish Prime Ministry Ottoman Archives has released a range of records related to the treatment of Ottoman Armenians during World War I. These include the texts of the aforementioned two cipher telegrams of 1916 and 1917, some of the responses to those telegrams, and a range of other records related to the deportation of Armenians. These new archival materials, though incomplete, demonstrate Talaat's intimate involvement with the deportation of Armenians, and show that his personal report on the Armenian Genocide was based on the results of his circular of 11 February 1917.

For example, soon after the first deportations in 1915, Talaat requested and received telegraphic and written reports of the number of people deported from different areas. In the case of Sivas (central kaza), for example, 21,446 Armenians (4,453 households) were deported from a population of 26,895 Armenians (5,032 households) and 5,449 Armenians (579 households) remained behind.[9] According to these figures, around 80 percent of Armenians had been deported from the center of the province. For the province as a whole, it was reported that 136,084 Armenians had been deported, with an additional 6,055 prepared for deportation.[10] In Kayseri, 44,271 were said to have been deported from a reported Armenian population of 49,947 people. Also, 765 deportees were reported as rearrested after escaping and returning back to Kayseri. The Kayseri report also added that the remaining 4,911 Armenians were earmarked to be scattered in Muslim villages so that they would not make more than five percent of the population in any locality.[11] Another report from Janik, on the Black Sea coast, reported that 25,476 Armenians (4,229 households) had been deported out of 27,453 Armenians (4,251 households).[12] According to these figures, the deportation rate from this Black Sea province by the end of 1915 was over 72 percent.[13] These initial reports from 1915 did not elaborate on the status of those who remained behind and we do not know how many of them were men who had been conscripted into the Ottoman army or Armenian converts to Islam.

The flow of information continued with special instructions from the Ottoman capital and local assessments of deportations. Fourteen months after the general deportations had begun, Talaat's circular of 24 August 1916, and then his circular of 11 February 1917, solicited new data concerning Armenians: while the August circular requested information based on local records dealing with the deportation of Armenians, the February circular asked for a new count in each area. Both circulars asked the central question about the number of "native" and "outside" Armenians in each province, but they differed in the additional details they requested. The August circular asked about Armenians who had not been deported because they were Catholics or Protestants, members of soldiers' families (*asker ailesi*), converts to Islam, or had special permission to remain;[14] the February circular asked for additional information on the geographical origins of "outside Armenians" in each province.

The responses to the August 1916 circular gave Talaat an overall reassessment of the results of his "deportation" program.[15] In the case of Kayseri, for example, this latest set of results maintained that 6,761 Armenians remained from a prewar population of over 50,000 Armenians.[16] According to these figures, around 77 percent of Armenians had been deported from this region.[17] In the case of Hudavendigar (Bursa) province, 2,999 Armenians remained from a prewar population of over 60,000.[18] According to these figures, around 95 percent of Armenians had been deported from Hudavendigar. In the case of Marash, of 39,901 Armenians,[19] there remained 2,442 Apostolic Armenians, 2,028 Catholic Armenians, and 1,813 Protestant Armenians, as well as 290 converts to Islam. According to these figures, by the end of 1916, 84 percent of Armenians had been deported from this region.[20] In the European province of Edirne, where there had been over 19,000 Armenians in 1914, only 4,583 people remained by the end of 1916.[21] Approximately 77 percent had been deported.

Six months later, the 11 February 1917 circular yielded more data that, as we argue, formed the basis of Talaat Pasha's report on the Armenian Genocide. In the case of Kastamonu, for example, the returns stated that there were 3,436 native and 188 outside Armenians. These figures were broken by gender with 1,177 male and 2,259 female "native" Armenians, and 29 male and 159 female "outside" Armenians. Regarding total numbers, the data from the 1917 survey was practically the same in Talaat's report, which noted 3,437 native and 185 outside Armenians in Kastamonu.[22] The return from Ankara province counted 12,766 native and 451 outside Armenians. Talaat's report gave the figures of 12,766 and 410 people.[23] The figures for Bolu were 1,608 native Armenians and 549 outsiders.[24] Talaat's report noted 1,539 locals and 551 outsiders. In the case of Karesi, the return reported 1,852 native and 246 outsiders. Talaat's report recorded 1,852 native and 124 outsiders.[25] In Beirut, the return counted 50 native and 1,980 outside Armenians. Talaat's report noted 50 natives and 1,849 outsiders.[26] In the case of Syria, the 1917 return counted 39,400 outside and no native Armenians.[27] Talaat's report gave the figures of 39,409 outsiders and no native Armenians. These sets of data show that Talaat's report was closely related to 11 February 1917 circular. The data appears to have been checked and updated using additional information.

Talaat's entry for Der Zor is particularly revealing. It recorded 201 native and 1,570 outside Armenians, and then amended the figure for outside Armenians to 6,778 in a footnote citing "additional telegraphic information."[28] Similarly, it recorded 10,703 outside Armenians for Aleppo based on the register that was sent from the province, but a note pointed out that telegraphic information from Aleppo had put the number of outside Armenians at 13,591.[29] The fact that such corrections occurred in footnotes, with explanations, supports our assertion that the 1917 report was based on a specific body of data, which were checked for some degree of accuracy. On the other hand, there appear to be some minor errors of arithmetic in the report: the detailed figures for Syria actually add up to 39,837 and not 39,409 as noted, and those for Mosul add up to 7,025 and not 7,033.[30]

Talaat's Perspective of the Armenian Genocide

Talaat was clearly aware of the destruction of Armenians while the deportations were in progress, and his report of 1917 was probably an effort to have a consolidated view of developments. His report was actually based on data from 23 regions of the Ottoman Empire, all, except for Hudavendigar, recipients of his circular of 11 February 1917.[31] The only province that did not respond to this circular was Jerusalem. These provinces were chosen for the survey because they still had residual Armenian populations, or they were areas where deportees had been sent in 1915–16. Consequently, the eastern provinces of Erzerum, Bitlis, Van, Diyarbekir, Trebizond, Elazig, and Janik were probably not included in the survey because they had been ordered to clear out their Armenian populations in 1915-16.[32]

When making his final calculations, Talaat used his data to account for Armenians in 29 Ottoman provinces.[33] Using population statistics for the distribution of Ottoman Armenians in 1914 and his 1917 statistics, Talaat could see the number and proportion of Armenians who had been deported in 1915-16 and estimate the number of those who had survived such deportations. According to Talaat's report, over one million Ottoman Armenians had disappeared between 1914 and 1917, with the remaining population divided amongst those who were resident in Constantinople (and were not deported), and those who were "natives" and "outsiders" in the provinces. Practically all who were "outsiders" were remnants of those who had been removed from their native provinces in 1915–16,[34] while "native" Armenians were those who were not deported outside of their home provinces – but may have been internally displaced within their native province.

The data in the 1917 report would have been interpreted in a more informed manner by Talaat Pasha, who had privileged knowledge about the Armenian issue. For example, he knew that tens of thousands of Armenians were destined for assimilation, such as women and children in Muslim households (see map p. 79). Thousands of other Armenians had also been scattered in central and western provinces to be absorbed into Muslim communities. Talaat knew that many Armenians had managed to escape from the Ottoman Empire, such as those who resisted Ottoman forces in Van in April 1915, as well as those who managed to flee across the Russian border in 1915–16. The number of people who escaped was probably around 150,000, and their ultimate survival was by no means clear. Thousands subsequently perished from privation and disease.

In the final analysis, the great majority of Ottoman Armenians were deported in 1915, and the great majority of these deportees were killed off through forced marches, privations, and outright massacres – as

THE DESTRUCTION OF ARMENIANS IN THE OTTOMAN EMPIRE, 1914–17

The View from Constantinople, 1917

This map represents Talaat Pasha's working data on the destruction of Ottoman Armenians in 1914–1917

KEY

Ottoman Armenians...

- % counted in native province in 1917
- % counted in other provinces in 1917
- % unaccounted in 1917

Data has not been adjusted for undercounts

No data from province in 1917

Size of circle relative to population size
For full data see *Talaat Pasha's Report on the Armenian Genocide.*

Official resettlement zone for Armenian deportees

Total number of Armenians shown on map 1,032,614

9% — 97,247 Armenians counted in native provinces in 1917

9% — 94,206 Armenians deported and accounted for elsewhere in 1917

82% — 841,161 Armenians unaccounted for in 1917

These figures have not been adjusted for undercounts, and the absence of Catholic and Protestant Armenians. According to Talaat's report, all figures should be increased by 30%.

© Ara Sarafian, 2022

Gomidas Institute

SURVIVING ARMENIAN DEPORTEES IN THE OTTOMAN EMPIRE, 1917

The View from Constantinople, 1917

This map represents
Talaat Pasha's working
data on the destruction
of Ottoman Armenians
in 1914-1917

KEY

Ottoman Armenians...

● % native to province 1917
● % outsider to provinces in 1917

Data has not been adjusted
for undercounts

Size of circle relative to population size
For full data see *Talaat Pasha's Report
on the Armenian Genocide*

Official resettlement zone
for Armenian deportees, 1915

Gomidas
Institute

© Ara Sarafian, 2022

Armenians counted
in 1917 (204,157)

52%
106,910 Armenians
from outside
provinces

48%
97,247
Armenians
native to
provinces

These figures have not been adjusted for undercounts.

* The data for Der Zor on this map represents the uncorrected figure that appeared
in Talaat's main report, and not the adjusted figure in his footnotes.

Black Sea

Mediterranean Sea

Van
Lake Van
Erzerum
Bitlis
Trebizond
Mamuret-ul
Aziz
Diyarbekir
Janik
Sivas   10% / 90%
Marash   3% / 97%
Urfa   15% / 85%
Kastamonu   5% / 95%
Kayseri   2% / 98%
Nigde   19% / 81%
Adana   26% / 74%
Ankara   3% / 97%
Bolu   26% / 74%
Konia   32% / 68%
Ichil   32% / 68%
Izmit   96% / 4%
Eskishehir   47% / 53%
Afyon Karahisar 44% / 56%
Kutahya   85% / 15%
Hudavendigar 94% / 6%
Karesi   94% / 6%
Aydin   67% / 33%
Teke (Antalya)
Menteshe
Constantinople
Chatalja
Edirne
Kaza-i Sultaniye (Gallipoli) 94% / 6%
Aleppo   50% / 50%
Beirut   97% / 3%
Syria   100%
Der Zor*   97% / 3%
Mosul   97% / 3%
Baghdad

attested and corroborated by eyewitness accounts.[35] Talaat's report clearly shows that the deportation of Ottoman Armenians in 1915 was part of an effort that aimed at the destruction of Armenians. The object of the authorities was not a population transfer (*tehcir*) but the destruction of entire communities. This fact is quite apparent in the organization, implementation, and outcome of Talaat's policies, as can be seen in the discrepancy between the number of Armenians who were deported, and the number of deportees who were found in the resettlement zone in 1917. Talaat was well aware of this discrepancy since he closely supervised deportations throughout 1915–16. As his 1917 report shows, although over a million Armenians were deported, around 60,000 were counted in the resettlement zone outlined by the Ottoman government in and around Der Zor, another 50,000 were found dispersed along deportation routes, and around 100,000 were located within their home provinces. Practically all of these survivors in the provinces were treated as captives and pressured to assimilate as Muslim-Turks.

Talaat obviously considered the ruin of Ottoman Armenians a personal triumph and took his report into exile when he fled the Ottoman Empire in 1918. His report was not meant for public disclosure and may well have been destroyed were it not for Talaat's untimely death in 1921.

Presenting Talaat's Report on the Armenian Genocide

In the following pages we present Talaat's own understanding of the destruction of Armenians with a presentation of his personal report on the destruction of Armenians. This is the closest official overview we have of the Armenian Genocide according to Ottoman records.

In presenting Talaat's data, we have reorganized the body of information to show the distribution of Armenians according to their native provinces and then by their location in 1917. Such a presentation of Talaat's data allows us to see, as Talaat saw, details of how many Armenians had survived the deportations from different provinces in 1917. Such calculations were also included in Talaat's opening summary analysis.

Where the 1917 report did not include returns from particular provinces with Armenian populations, i.e., Edirne, Chatalja, Kala-i Sultaniye (Chanakkale), Janik and Jerusalem, we created special entries for those provinces and indicated the presence of Armenians from those areas in other parts of the Ottoman Empire covered by Talaat's report of 1917. When doing so, we indicated the number of Armenians in those provinces in 1914 based on official Ottoman sources. Such information would have been known to Talaat Pasha and figured into his own assessment of his report.

We also consolidated stray pieces of additional information into the report's chosen format, noting the original information in brackets or in footnotes. For example, some returns identified people as natives of Gallipoli or Hakkiari, which should have been counted as natives of Edirne or Van vilayets. In such cases we included the people concerned as natives of their respective vilayets, noting their additional details concerning Gallipoli or Hakkiari in brackets.

Some Armenians were identified in different provinces without giving details of their places of origin in the Ottoman Empire. Specifically, in Konia, 236 people were identified as employees of benevolent organisations and 216 as artisans. In Adana, 1,152 people were identified as working in the Taurus construction zone. In Aydin, 113 people were identified as "foreign nationals." In Beirut, one person was listed from Tiflis, two from Dedeagach, four from Filibe, and seven from Varna. In Sivas, three people were recorded from Salonika. In Ankara, one person was from Egypt and one from the Caucasus.

Readers might note the difference between the column showing 94,206 Armenians who were classed as living outside their native province, and the 106,910 who were listed as people from outside the province in which they were counted. The former figure is smaller because its information is limited to people from 29 provinces, while the latter figure is for people from all provinces, in addition to Armenians who were simply identified as outsiders, such as workers in the "Taurus construction zone," "artisans," or "foreigners."

All information presented in the following pages is derived from Talaat's original report. All additional comments, including titles to sections, are placed in square brackets, footnotes or clearly marked as "appended." No information was left out from the original report. The two appendixes at the back also relate to Talaat's report. While the first appendix provides more substance to the disappearance of Armenians, the second appendix, Talaat's "Black Book," carries the embedded authority of being Talaat's private report and reflecting his broader genocidal predisposition in terms of favoring the Muslim population of the Ottoman Empire and liquidating Christian Armenian and Greek communities.

Endnotes

1. 8 August 1915 diary entry of conversation between Talaat Pasha and U.S. Ambassador Henry Morgenthau, *United States Diplomacy on the Bosphorus: The Diaries of Ambassador Morgenthau, 1913–1916*, comp., ed., and intro. Ara Sarafian, London: Gomidas Institute, 2022.

2. See cipher telegram dated 24 August 1916, Sublime Porte, Constantinople, Talat Pasha to Edirne, Adana, Ankara, Aydin, Bitlis, Baghdad, Beirut, Aleppo, Hudavendigar, Diyarbekir, Syria, Sivas, Trebizond, Kastamonu, Konia, Mamuretulaziz, Mosul, Urfa, Izmit, Bolu, Janik, Zor, Karesi, Jerusalem, Kala-i Sultaniye, Menteshe, Teke, Kayseri, Karahisar Sahib, Ichil, Kutahya, Marash, Nigde, Eskishehir, DH.Şfr, 68/112. Note: all archival citations are from the Ottoman Prime Ministry Archives (Istanbul) unless otherwise stated.

3. See cipher telegram dated Sublime Porte, Directorate of Public Security, Constantinople, 11 Feb. 1917, Talaat Pasha to Adana, Ankara, Aydin, Beirut, Aleppo, Syria, Sivas, Kastamonu, Konia, Mosul, Urfa, Izmit, Eskishehir, Ichil, Bolu, Zor, Karasi, Jerusalem, Kayseri, Afyon Karahissar, Kutahya, Marash and Nigde. See DH.Şfr., 72/210.

4. Murat Bardakçı, *Talat Paşa'nın Evrak-ı Metrukesi : Sadrazam Talat Paşa'nın özel arşivinde bulunan Ermeni tehciri konusundaki belgeler ve hususi yazışmalar* [The Remaining Documents of Talaat Pasha: Documents and Important Correspondence Found in the Private Archives of Sadrazam Talaat Pasha about the Armenian Deportations], Istanbul: Everest Yayınları, 2008. This publication appeared in parts in "Talat Paşa'nın Kara Kaplı Defteri" in *Hürriyet*, 24-27 April 2005; "Paşa'ya göre Ermeni Sayıları", *Hürriyet*, 26 Sept. 2005; "Talat Paşa'nın Tehcir Belgeleri", *Hürriyet*, 23-26 April, 2006; and "Talat Paşa, Elazığ'dan 74 bin,206 Ermeni'nin tehcir edildiğini yazıyor," *Sabah*, 26 Feb. 2007.

5. Bardakçı, *Talat Paşa'nın Evrak-ı Metrukesi*, p. 12.

6. Two major provinces were left out of Talaat's summary account: Edirne vilayet and Janik mutasarriflik.

7. See Bardakçı, *Talat Paşa'nın Evrak-ı Metrukesi*, p. 109. According to Talaat's notes, the figure of 1,500,000 was made up of Apostolic and Catholic Armenians in all of the Ottoman Empire. The figure of 350,000–400,000 probably included Protestant Armenians as well because during the deportations of 1915–16 they were treated as Armenians by Ottoman officials. Some exemptions were granted, often temporary ones, to exclude Catholic and Protestant Armenians from deportations. These were invariably cases of placating Western powers. For example, this was the case in

Erzerum, where Catholic and Protestant Armenians were also deported soon after the main body of Apostolic Armenians were sent away. See EUM.2 Şb. 10/23 dated 6 L 1333 (18 Aug. 1915).

8. Bardakçı, *Talat Paşa'nın Evrak-ı Metrukesi,* p. 109. Talaat's figures represented the perspective at the Ottoman government, and that is our central focus for this study.

9. EUM.2Şb., 73/44, dated 16 Z 1333 (27 Sept. 1915). These figures may have included soldiers conscripted into the Ottoman army, as more men were left behind than women. The deported were made up of 11,590 females and 8,856 males, while those who remained behind were listed as 1,694 females and 3,755 males.

10. EUM.2 Şb., 68/84 dated 28 Sept. 1915.

11. EUM.2 Şb., 68/75 dated 18 Sept. 1915.

12. EUM.2 Şb., 73/53. This document has been dated as "30 Za 1333" by the archives, though the original date on the report reads "24 Eylul 1331 (Rumi)" which translates to 7 Oct. 1915.

13. EUM.2 Şb., 73/53, dated 33 Za. 1329 (10 Oct. 1915).

14. All of these were contested categories of survivors. Some Catholic and Protestant Armenians were given exemption from deportations because of foreign intervention, though most Catholics and Protestants were actually deported between 1915 and 1917. While family members of Armenian soldiers serving in the Ottoman army were supposed to be exempted from deportations, many were actually deported or scattered into Muslim villages for assimilation. Some Armenians converted to Islam to avoid deportation, though often they too were deported, or expected to intermarry with non-Armenians.

15. The terminology used to describe the removal of Armenians was either *sefkiyat* (despatch, expulsion) and *iskan* (settlement).

16. According to official Ottoman statistics for 1914, there were 48,659 Apostolic Armenians, 1,515 Catholic Armenians, and 2,018 Protestants (mainly Armenians) in the mutasarriflik of Kayseri. See *Arşiv Belgeleriyle Ermeni Faalilyetleri,* vol 1, p. 624. For the number of Armenians counted in the province, see EUM.2 Şb., 74/28, dated 25 Z 1334 (24 Aug. 1916). According to this document these remaining Armenians were composed of 3,430 "native" Armenians, 11 "outside" Armenians, 634 Catholic Armenians, 507 Protestant Armenians, 2,060 members of "soldiers' families", and 115 converts to Islam.

17. These figures were comparable, in gross terms, to the earlier report from 18 Sept. 1915.

18. According to official Ottoman figured for 1914, there were 58,921

Apostolic Armenians, 1,278 Catholic Armenians, and 992 Protestants (mostly Armenians) in Hudavendigar province. See *Arşiv Belgeleriyle Ermeni Faaliyetleri*, vol 1, p. 611. For the number of remaining Armenians see EUM.2 Şb., 74/29, dated 3 M 1335 (31 Oct. 1916). According to this document the remaining 2,999 Armenians were composed of 84 "native" Armenians, 1,136 Catholic Armenians, 1,032 Protestant Armenians, 536 members of "soldiers' [and officials'] families," 52 converts to Islam, and 159 people who remained by special permission.

19. The official figure for Armenians in Marash in 1914 was 37,416, See *Arşiv Belgelerle*, p. 655.

20. EUM.2 Şb., 74/24, dated 20 Z. 1334 (19.10.1916).

21. According to official sources, on the eve of World War I there had been 19,523 Apostolic Armenians, 248 Catholic Armenians, and 115 Protestants belonging to different ethnic communities. See *Arşiv Belgeleriyle Ermeni Faalilyetleri*, vol 1, p. 613. For the number of remaining Armenians see EUM.2 Şb., 74/36, dated 22 M 1335 (19 Nov. 1916).

22. EUM.2 Şb., 74/66, dated 10 Ş. 1335 (10 June 1917). This archival document also gave a detailed breakdown of its data to the level of kazas and by gender. For example, it shows 66 percent of local Armenians and 85 percent of outside Armenians in the province were women.

23. EUM.2 Şb., 75/46. This document is not dated on the original.

24. EUM.2 Şb., 74/52, dated 16 Ca 1335 (10 March 1917).

25. EUM.2 Şb., 74/53, dated 17 Ca 1335 (11 March 1917).

26. EUM.2 Şb., 74/57, dated 23 Ca 1335 (17 March 1917).

27. EUM.2 Şb., 74/58, dated 28 Ca 1335 (22 March 1917).

28. Unfortunately, none of the relevant correspondence related to the figures for Zor could be located in the Prime Ministry Ottoman Archives by this author.

29. Bardakçı, *Talat Paşa'nın Evrak-ı Metrukesi*, pp. 132-133.

30. See Bardakçı, *Talat Paşa'nın Evrak-ı Metrukesi*, pp. 128–29 and pp. 138–39. (The body of our data in this study reflects the detailed figures, except for the summary page, which has been left as in the original).

31. The provinces in question were the vilayets of Eskishehir, Adana, Sivas, Beirut, Kastamonu, Konia, Aydin, Syria, Hudavendigar, Aleppo, Ankara, Mosul and the mutasarrifliks of Izmit, Kutahya, Bolu, Karahisar-i Sahib, Ichil, Karesi, Kayseri, Marash, Zor, Nigde, Urfa.

32. For the telegram ordering the complete deportation of Armenians from Erzerum, Van, and Bitlis, see Talaat Pasha's circular to Erzerum, Van, and Bitlis provinces dated Constantinople, 10 May 1915 in EUM.DH.Şfr, 53/93; For the complete deportation of Armenians from Trebizond, Mamuretulaziz,

Sivas, Diyarbekir, and Janik, see Talaat Pasha to provinces dated Constantinople, 20 June 1915, EUM.DH.Şfr 54/87. For an example of one interim report claiming that there were no Armenians left in Janik, Trebizond, Erzerum, or Bitlis see "Appendix I" to this work. There were reportedly no more Armenians left in Diyarbekir, nor any in Mamuretulaziz, save for 4,000 women and children hiding in villages by the end of 1915. See EUM.2 Şb., 68/72 and 68/70 dated 18 Sept. 1915. Likewise, when Talaat ordered a halt to deportations in 1916, none of the eastern provinces were included on the list of recipients, presumably because there were no Armenians left in those regions. See EUM.2 Şb., 62/21, dated 15 March 1916.

33. These were the 23 provinces that sent data for the report, plus Erzerum, Bitlis, Van, Diyarbekir, Trebizond and Mamuretulaziz which were supposed to have no Armenian inhabitants in 1917.

34. Talaat's summary notes that 68,433 Armenians lived outside their native provinces in 1914 (e.g., as migrant workers). By all accounts, such Armenians fared as other Armenians of their host communities. Where members of this class of people were not deported in 1915–16, they would still have been classified as "outsiders" in their places of abode. If they were deported and survived, their native province would have been registered as their original provinces and not where they came from. For example, of 3,364 Armenians from Erzerum counted in 1917, those found in Mosul and Syria (1,662) were certainly deportees, those in Izmir (481) were certainly migrant workers, while the status of those in Urfa, Aleppo, or Sivas (1,035 people) is more difficult to determine.

35. The abuse and murder of Armenians was recorded by foreign observers and Armenian survivors. In the Harpoot (Kharpert) region, for example, we have the private papers of local Christian missionaries and foreign consular staff, as well as the memoirs of survivors. See Maria Jacobsen, *Diaries of a Danish Missionary. Harpoot, 1907-1919*, Princeton and London: Gomidas Institute, 2001; Henry H. Riggs, *Days of Tragedy in Armenia: Personal Experiences in Harpoot*, 1915-1917, Princeton, NJ: Gomidas Institute, 1997; Tacy Atkinson, *The German, the Turk and the Devil Made a Triple Alliance: Harpoot Diaries, 1908-1917*, Princeton, NJ: Gomidas Institute, 2000; James Barton, *"Turkish Atrocities": Statements of American Missionaries on the Destruction of Christian Communities in Ottoman Turkey*, 1915-1917, Princeton, NJ: Gomidas Institute, 1998; Hampartzoum Mardiros Chitjian, *A Hair's Breadth from Death*, London: Gomidas Institute, 2021; and the report of US Consul Leslie A. Davis in *United States Official Records on the Armenian Genocide, 1915-1917*, comp., ed. and intro by Ara Sarafian, London: Gomidas Institute, 2019.

TALAAT PASHA'S REPORT ON THE ARMENIAN GENOCIDE, 1917

SURVEY OF OTTOMAN

Provinces informing Talaat Pasha's report in 1917.

Eastern provinces which were not included in Talaat's 1917 population survey of Armenians.*

- - - - - - 'Resettlement zone' as indicated in Talaat Pasha's 'black book.'

* These provinces were probably not included in the survey because no Armenians were supposed to remain there after the 1915 deportations. Talaat's 1917 survey showed that the vast majority of deportees from these provinces had disappeared by 1917. See the mapping of Talaat's data on page 10, as well as the official Turkish denialist position today on page 73.

ARMENIANS, FEBRUARY 1917

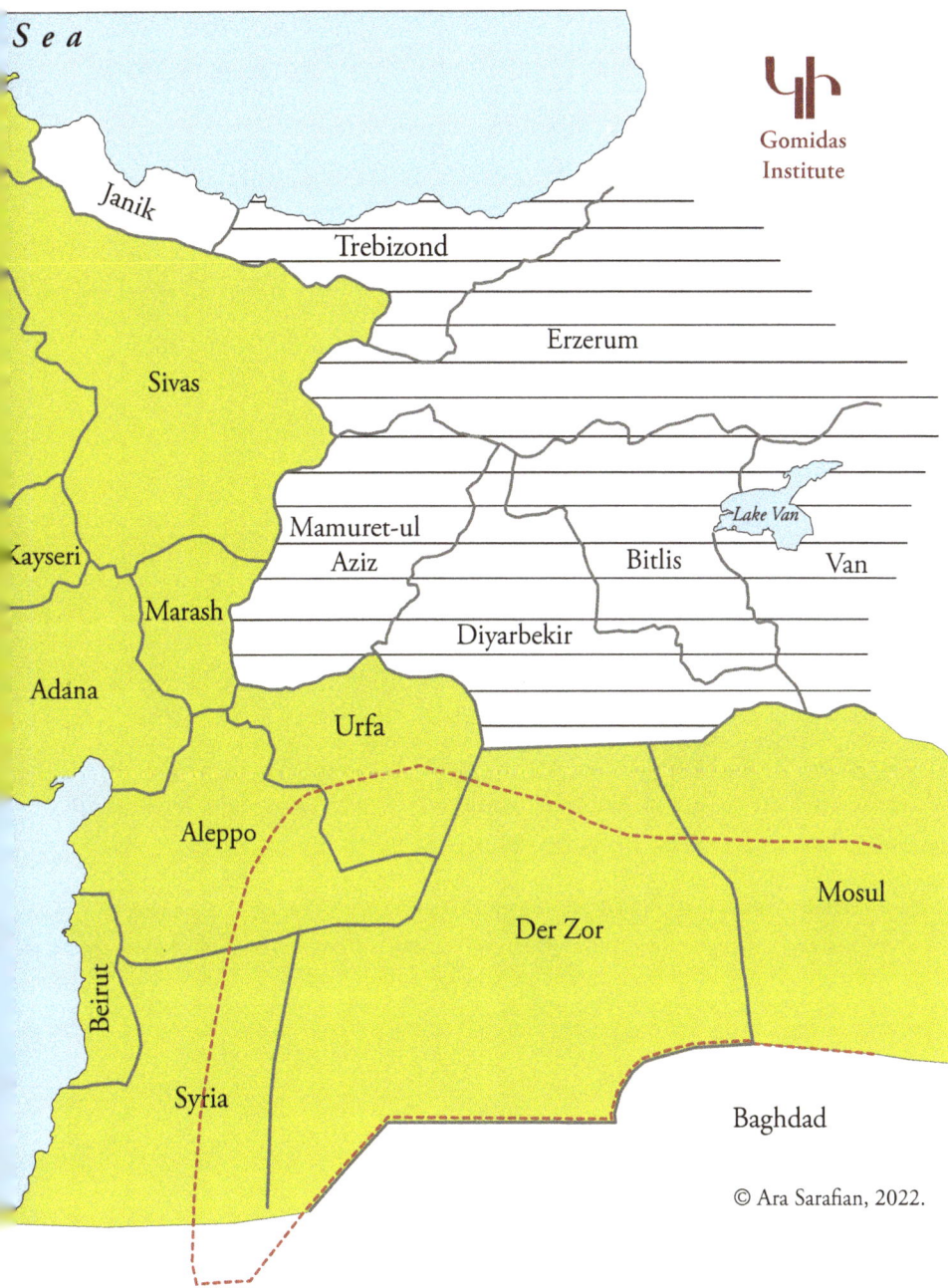

S e a

Janik

Trebizond

Erzerum

Sivas

Mamuret-ul
Aziz

Lake Van

Bitlis

Van

Kayseri

Marash

Diyarbekir

Adana

Urfa

Aleppo

Mosul

Beirut

Der Zor

Syria

Baghdad

Gomidas
Institute

© Ara Sarafian, 2022.

[Original Notes to Opening Summary Page (opposite)][*]

[*]. This figure is reflected in the total number of outside Armenians.

[**]. There were 68,433 Armenians who lived outside their native provinces in 1914.

[NOTE] The number of Gregorian [Apostolic] Armenians in the 1914 census is 1,187,818 and Armenian Catholics 63,967 bringing their total to 1,256,403 [sic]. Because of the incomplete nature of the data, the true figure for these communities should be around 1,500,000. The number of Armenians who are today counted as locals and outsiders [including those of Constantinople] is 284,157 and this figure should be increased by 30 percent bringing their number to around 350,000 to 400,000.

---

[1] Bardakçı, *Talaat Paşa'nın Evrak-ı Metrukesi*, pp. 108 and 109. This executive summary is at the beginning of Talaat's report. It reflects the rationale of the entire report – the destruction of Armenians at a provincial level.

[2] Some provinces which had Armenian populations are missing among those listed in Talaat's report. These are Edirne, Chatalja, Kale-i Sultaniye (Chanakkale), Menteshe, Teke (Antalya), Janik, Kudus (Jerusalem). Although the report gives a figure of 80,000 Armenians in Constantinople in 1917, this is an approximation and does not include a breakdown in the main body of the report.

[Opening Summary Page: Data and Calculations][1]

Province[2] [vilayet/ mutasarriflik]	Native Armenians in province	Outside Armenians in province	Armenians of province in other provinces	Armenians in 1914
Ankara	12,766	410	4,560	44,661
Mosul	253	7,033	0	0
Nigde	193	850	547	4,939
Izmit	3,880	142	9,464	56,115
Kutahya	3,932	680	0	4,023
Eskishehir	1,258	1,096	1,104	8,620
Bolu	1,539	551	56	3,002
Afyon Karahisar	2,234	1,778	1,484	7,498
Ichil	252	116	0	350
Karesi	1,852	124	1,696	8,663
Kayseri	6,650	111	6,778	47,974
Adana	12,263	4,257	19,664	51,723
Marash	6,115	198	2,010	27,306
Sivas	8,097	948	3,993	141,000
Beirut	50	1,849	0	1,224
Kastamonu	3,437	185	211	9,052
Konia	3,730	14,210	3,639	13,078
Aydin	11,901	5,729	0	19,710
Syria	0	39,409	0	0
Zor	201	6,778	0	63
Hudavendigar	2,821	178	10,251	59,038
Aleppo	13,679	13,591	19,091	37,031
Urfa	1,144	6,687	451	15,616
Erzerum	0	0	3,364	125,657
Bitlis	0	0	1,061	114,704
Van	0	0	160	67,792
Diyarbekir	0	0	1,849	56,166
Trebizond	0	0	562	37,549
Mamuretulaziz (Elaziz)	0	0	2,201	70,060
	----------	----------	----------	----------------
	97,247	106,910	94,206 [*]	1,032,614
Istanbul	80,000	0	0	80,000
	----------	----------	----------	----------------
[Natives 1917]	177,247	106,910	94,206	1,112,614 [**]
[Outsiders 1917]	106,910			

[Total 1917]	284,157			

APPENDED

WESTERN PROVINCES

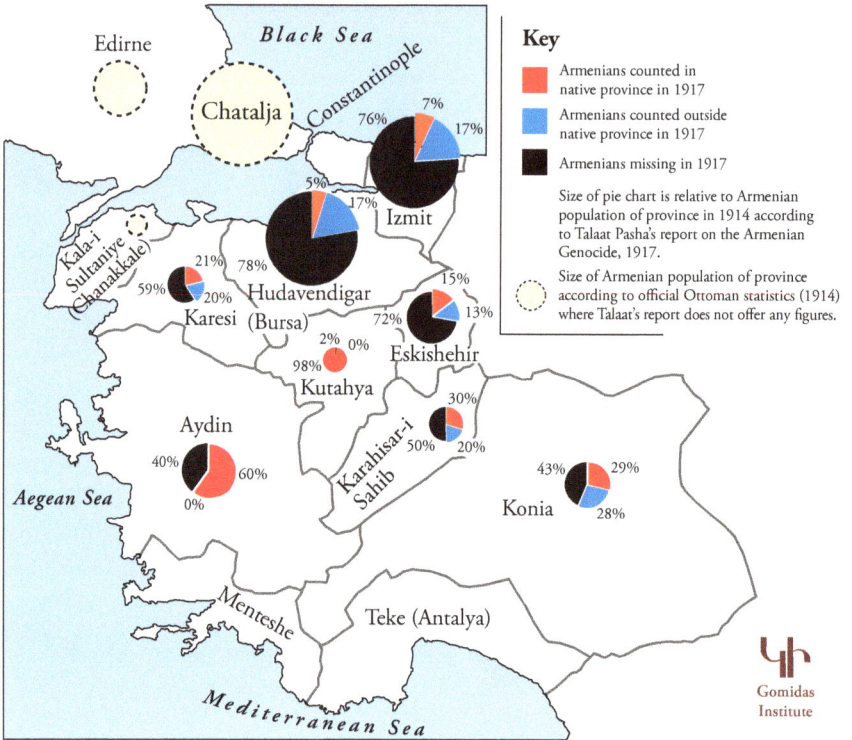

Edirne

Black Sea

Chatalja

Constantinople

Key

■ Armenians counted in native province in 1917

■ Armenians counted outside native province in 1917

■ Armenians missing in 1917

Size of pie chart is relative to Armenian population of province in 1914 according to Talaat Pasha's report on the Armenian Genocide, 1917.

Size of Armenian population of province according to official Ottoman statistics (1914) where Talaat's report does not offer any figures.

7%
76%
17%

Izmit

5%
17%

Kala-i Sultaniye (Chanakkale)

21% 78%
59% 20%

Hudavendigar

Karesi (Bursa)

2% 0%
98%

Kutahya

15%
72% 13%

Eskishehir

30%
50% 20%

Karahisar-i Sahib

43% 29%
28%

Konia

Aydin

40% 60%
0%

Aegean Sea

Menteshe   Teke (Antalya)

Mediterranean Sea

Gomidas Institute

CONSTANTINOPLE[*]

Distribution of Constantinople Armenians in 1917

Constantinople (native)   n/i

Adana	72
Afyonkarahisar	3
Ankara	18
Aydin	616
Beirut	54
Bolu	48
Eskishehir	73
Aleppo	73
Izmit	38
Karesi	3
Kastamonu	21
Kayseri	3
Konia	230
Kutahya	4
Mosul	9
Sivas	5
Syria	13
Urfa	5
Zor	20
TOTAL	1,308

Talaat Pasha's Summary Data

Native Armenians of vilayet (1914)	n/i [†]
Native Armenians in vilayet (1917)	n/i
Native Armenians outside vilayet (1917)	1,308
Missing native Armenian population (1917)	n/i

---

[*] There was no separate return for Constantinople in Talaat Pasha's report. The data presented here was gathered from the returns of the 23 other provinces that appeared in the report.

[†] According to official Ottoman population statistics for 1914, there were 82,880 Apostolic and Catholic Armenians in Istanbul. Protestant Armenians were not counted separately and have been left out of our calculations. See T. C. Genelkurmay Başkanlığı, *Arşiv Belgeleriyle*, vol. 1, p. 605.

EDIRNE VILAYET[*]

Distribution of Edirne Armenians in 1917

Edirne (native)	n/i	
Adana	95	
Afyonkarahisar	16	
Aydin	137	
Beirut	6	
Bolu	4	
Eskishehir	16	
Izmit	6	(from Gallipoli)
Karesi	9	(from Gallipoli)
Konia	90	
Mosul	87	(from Rodosto)
Nigde	8	
Sivas	1	
Syria	677	
Zor	38	
TOTAL	1,190	

Talaat Pasha's Summary Data

Native Armenians of vilayet (1914)	n/i [†]
Native Armenians in vilayet (1917)	n/i
Native Armenians outside vilayet (1917)	1,190
Missing native Armenian population (1917)	n/i

---

[*] There was no separate return for Edirne in Talaat Pasha's report. The data presented here was gathered from the returns of the 23 other provinces that appeared in the report.

[†] According to official Ottoman population statistics for 1914, there were 19,771 Apostolic (19,523) and Catholic Armenians (248) in Edirne. See *Arşiv Belgeleriyle*, p. 613.

CHATALJA MUTASARRIFLIK[*]
Distribution of Chatalja Armenians in1917

Chatalja (native)	n/i
Aydin	3
Karesi	5
TOTAL	8

Talaat Pasha's Summary Data

Native Armenians of vilayet (1914)	n/i [†]
Native Armenians in vilayet (1917)	n/i
Native Armenians outside vilayet (1917)	8
Missing native Armenian population (1917)	n/i

---

[*] There was no return for Chatalja in Talaat Pasha's report. The data presented here was gathered from the returns of the 23 other provinces that appeared in the report.
[†] According to official Ottoman population statistics for 1914, there were 842 Apostolic Armenians in Chatalja. See *Arşiv Belgeleriyle*, p. 605 and p. 617.

IZMIT MUTASARRIFLIK*
Distribution of Izmit Armenians in 1917

Izmit (native)	3,880	
Adana	82	
Afyonkarahisar	656	
Ankara	3	
Aydin	116	
Beirut	22	
Bolu	155	
Eskishehir	386	
Aleppo	862	
Konia	4,399	
Kutahya	300	
Mosul	607	
Nigde	776	
Syria	797	
Urfa	309	
Zor	85	
TOTAL	9,555	13,435

Talaat Pasha's Summary Data

Native Armenians of vilayet (1914)	56,115	
Native Armenians in vilayet (1917)	3,880	
Native Armenians outside vilayet (1917)	9,555	
Missing native Armenian population (1917)	42,680	(-76%)

---

* Talaat's report gave the following figures for Armenians by place of origin in Izmit in 1917: Izmit (native) 3,880; Istanbul 38; Van 24; Bitlis 22; Kayseri 14; Konia 14; Ankara 13; Gallipoli 6; Hudavendigar 5; Bolu 2; Elazig 2; Sivas 1; Trebizond 1. Total 4,022.

APPENDED

THE ARMENIAN GENOCIDE IN THE WESTERN PROVINCES

Armenians from each region counted in their native province, outside their native province, and missing in 1917

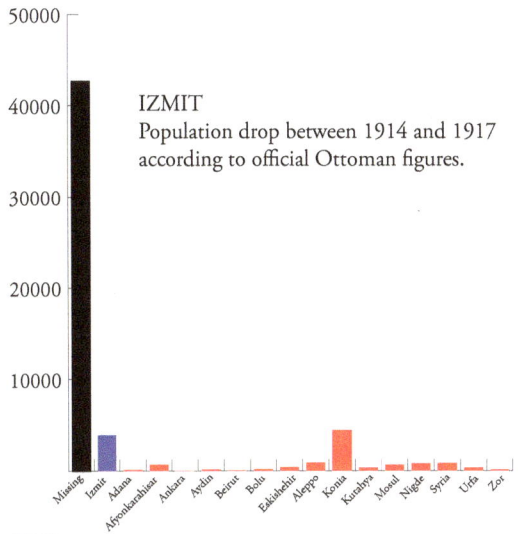

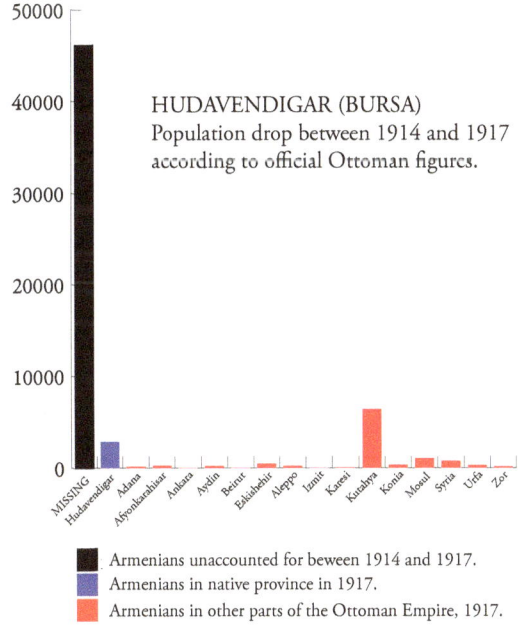

IZMIT
Population drop between 1914 and 1917
according to official Ottoman figures.

HUDAVENDIGAR (BURSA)
Population drop between 1914 and 1917
according to official Ottoman figures.

■ Armenians unaccounted for beween 1914 and 1917.
■ Armenians in native province in 1917.
■ Armenians in other parts of the Ottoman Empire, 1917.

Gomidas
Institute

HUDAVENDIGAR (BURSA) VILAYET[*]

Distribution of Hudavendigar Armenians in 1917

Hudavendigar (native) 2,821

Adana	131	
Afyonkarahisar	242	
Ankara	5	
Aydin	197	
Beirut	14	
Eskishehir	454	
Aleppo	192	
Izmit	5	
Karesi	18	
Konia	6,349	
Kutahya	301	
Mosul	1,012	
Syria	726	
Urfa	285	
Zor	130	
TOTAL	10,061	12,882

Talaat Pasha's Summary Data

Native Armenians of vilayet (1914)	59,038	
Native Armenians in vilayet (1917)	2,821	
Native Armenians outside vilayet (1917)	10,061	
Missing native Armenian population (1917)	46,156	(-78%)

---

[*] Talaat's report gave the following figures for Armenians by place of origin in Hudavendigar in 1917: Hudavendigar (native) 2,821; Kala-i Sultaniye 178. Total 2,999.

KARESI MUTASARRIFLIK[*]
Distribution of Karesi Armenians in 1917

Karesi (native)	1,852	
Adana	22	
Afyonkarahisar	115	
Aydin	100	
Beirut	9	
Eskishehir	9	
Aleppo	88	
Konia	966	
Nigde	20	
Syria	128	
Urfa	244	
Zor	22	
TOTAL	1,723	3,575

Talaat Pasha's Summary Data

Native Armenians of vilayet (1914)	8,663	
Native Armenians in vilayet (1917)	1,852	
Native Armenians outside vilayet (1917)	1,723	
Missing native Armenian population (1917)	5,088	(-59%)

---

[*] Talaat's report gave the following figures for Armenians by place of origin in Karesi in 1917: Karesi (native) 1,852; Van 28; Kala-i Sultaniye 22; Hudavendigar 18; Ankara 13; Erzerum 11; Gallipoli 9; Chatalja 5; Constantinople 3; Sivas 2; Konia 2; Aydin 2; Malatya 2; Kutahya 1; Eskishehir 1; Kayseri 1; Adana 1; Bitlis 1; Janik 1; Karahisar 1. Total 1,976.

KALA-I SULTANIYE MUTASARRIFLIK (CHANAKKALE)[*]
Distribution of Chanakkale Armenians in 1917

Kala-i Sultaniye (native)   n/i

Kutahya	6
Afyonkarahisar	10
Karesi	22
Kastamonu	5
Konia	7
Aydin	43
Syria	129
Zor	4
Hudavendigar	178
TOTAL	404

Talaat Pasha's Summary Data

Native Armenians of vilayet (1914)	n/i [†]
Native Armenians in vilayet (1917)	n/i
Native Armenians outside vilayet (1917)	404
Missing native Armenian population (1917)	n/i

---

[*] There was no separate return for Kala-i Sultaniye (Çanakkale) in Talaat Pasha's report. The data presented here was gathered from the returns of the 23 other provinces that appeared in the report.

[†] According to official Ottoman population statistics for 1914, there were 2,474 Apostolic Armenians in Kala-i Sultaniye. See *Arşiv Belgeleriyle*, p. 605.

ESKISHEHIR VILAYET[*]

Distribution of Eskishehir Armenians in 1917

Eskishehir (native)	1,258	
Ankara	20	
Beirut	4	
Aleppo	129	
Ichil	56	
Kayseri	1	
Konia	619	
Kutahya	62	
Mosul	30	
Nigde	1	
Syria	113	
Urfa	188	
Zor	5	
TOTAL	1,228	2,486

Talaat Pasha's Summary Data

Native Armenians of vilayet (1914)	8,620	
Native Armenians in vilayet (1917)	1,258	
Native Armenians outside vilayet (1917)	1,228	
Missing native Armenian population (1917)	6,134	(71%)

---

[*] Talaat's report gave the following figures for Armenians by place of origin in Eskishehir in 1917: Eskishehir (native) 1,258; Hudavendigar 454; Izmit 386; Constantinople 73; Ankara 62; Kutahya 46; Bitlis 21; Edirne 16; Afyon Karahissar12; Sivas 9; Karesi 9; Kayseri 8. Total 2,354.

AYDIN VILAYET[*]
Distribution of Aydin Armenians in 1917

Aydin (native)	11,901	
Adana	41	
Aleppo	34	
Ichil	6	
Karesi	2	
Konia	7	
Sivas	1	
Syria	21	
Zor	10	
TOTAL	122	12,023

Talaat Pasha's Summary Data

Native Armenians of vilayet (1914)	19,710	
Native Armenians in vilayet (1917)	11,901	
Native Armenians outside vilayet (1917)	122	
Missing native Armenian population (1917)	7,687	(-39%)

---

[*] Talaat's report gave the following figures for Armenians by place of origin in Aydin in 1917: Aydin (native) 11,901; Kayseri 1,600; Constantinople 616; Erzerum 481; Konia 383; Afyon Karahissar 371; Sivas 303; Bitlis 294; Elazig 254; Ankara 219; Hudavendigar 197; Edirne 137; Foreigners 133; Izmit 116; Kutahya 101; Karesi 100; Adana 78; Van 74; Diyarbekir 73; Marash 50; Aleppo 46; Trebizond 46; Kala-i Sultaniye 43; Urfa 29; Janik 21; Antalya 13; Menteshe 12; Kastamonu 9; Bolu 8; Nigde 7; Jerusalem 7; Beirut 6; Chatalja 3. Total 17,731.

KUTAHYA MUTASARRIFLIK[*]

Distribution of Kutahya Armenians in 1917

Kutahya (native)	3,932	
Aydin	101	
Eskishehir	46	
Karesi	1	
Kastamonu	2	
Konia	7	
TOTAL	157	4,089

Talaat Pasha's Summary Data

Native Armenians of vilayet (1914)	4,023
Native Armenians in vilayet (1917)	3,932
Native Armenians outside vilayet (1917)	157
Missing native Armenian population (1917)	none

---

[*] Talaat's report gave the following figures for Armenians by place of origin in Kutahya in 1917: Kutahya (native) 3,932; Hudavendigar 301; Izmit 300; Eskishehir 62; Kala-i Sultaniye 6; Konia 5; Istanbul 4; Ankara 2. Total 4,612.

AFYON KARAHISAR (KARAHISAR-I SÂHIB) MUTASARRIFLIK[*]
Distribution of Afyon Karahisar Armenians in 1917

Afyon Karahisar (native) 2,234

Aydin	371	
Beirut	17	
Eskishehir	12	
Aleppo	52	
Karesi	1	
Konia	502	
Syria	419	
Urfa	111	
Zor	19	
TOTAL	1,504	3,738

Talaat Pasha's Summary Data

Native Armenians of vilayet (1914)	7,498	
Native Armenians in vilayet (1917)	2,234	
Native Armenians outside vilayet (1917)	1,504	
Missing native Armenian population (1917)	3,760	(-50%)

---

[*] Talaat's report gave the following figures for Armenians by place of origin in Afyon Karahisar in 1917: Afyon Karahisar (native) 2,234; Ankara 578; Izmit 565; Hudavendigar 424; Karesi 115; Eskishehir 56; Edirne 16; Konia 11; Kala-i Sultaniye 10; Constantinople 3. Total 4,012.

KONIA VILAYET[*]
Distribution of Konia Armenians in 1917

Konia (native)	3,730	
Adana	207	
Afyonkarahisar	11	
Aydin	383	
Beirut	83	
Bolu	155	
Aleppo	469	
Ichil	15	
Izmit	14	
Karesi	2	
Kutahya	5	
Mosul	407	
Nigde	6	
Sivas	1	
Syria	1,525	
Urfa	311	
Zor	48	
TOTAL	3,642	7,372

Talaat Pasha's Summary Data

Native Armenians of vilayet (1914)	13,078	
Native Armenians in vilayet (1917)	3,730	
Native Armenians outside vilayet (1917)	3,642	
Missing native Armenian population (1917)	5,706	(-44%)

---

* Talaat's report gave the following figures for Armenians by place of origin in Konia in 1917: Konia (native) 3,730; Hudavendigar 6,349; Izmit 4,399; Ankara 1,518; Karesi 966; Eskishehir 619; Afyon Karahissar 502; Workers of **benevolent organisations** 236; Constantinople 230; Artisans 216; Edirne 90; Sivas 30; Kayseri 16; Kutahya 7; Aydin 7; Kala-i Sultaniye 7; Nigde 5; Kastamonu 3; Bitlis 3; Trebizond 2; Adana 1; Aleppo 1; Van 1; Elazig 1. Total 18,939.

MENTESHE MUTASARRIFLIK[*]
Distribution of Menteshe Armenians in 1917

Menteshe (native)	n/i	
Aydin	12	
TOTAL	12	n/i [†]

Talaat Pasha's Summary Data
Native Armenians of vilayet (1914)   n/i [‡]
Native Armenians in vilayet (1917)   n/i
Native Armenians outside vilayet (1917)   12
Missing native Armenian population (1917)   n/i

---

[*] There was no separate return for Menteshe in Talaat Pasha's report. The data presented here was gathered from the returns of the 23 other provinces that appeared in the report.

[†] According to a return to the August 1916 circular, there were 2 native and 51 outside Armenians in Menteshe. See EUM.2 Sb, 28/47-A dated 4 Z 1334 (3 Oct. 1916).

[‡] According to official Ottoman figures for 1914, there were 12 Apostolic Armenians in Menteşe. See *Arşiv Belgeleriyle...* p. 641.

TEKE (ANTALYA) MUTASARRIFLIK
Distribution of Teke Armenians ofin 1917

Teke (native)	n/i
Aydin	13
TOTAL	12 n/i *

Talaat Pasha's Summary Data
Native Armenians of vilayet (1914)   n/i †
Native Armenians in vilayet (1917)   n/i
Native Armenians outside vilayet (1917)   13
Missing native Armenian population (1917)   n/i

---

* There is no separate return recorded for Antalya (Teke) mutasarriflik in Talaat Pasha's report. The data presented here was gathered from the returns of the 23 other provinces that appear in his report.
† According to official Ottoman figures for 1914, there were 630 Apostolic Armenians in Antalya. See *Arşiv Belgeleriyle*, p. 661.

APPENDED

CENTRAL PROVINCES

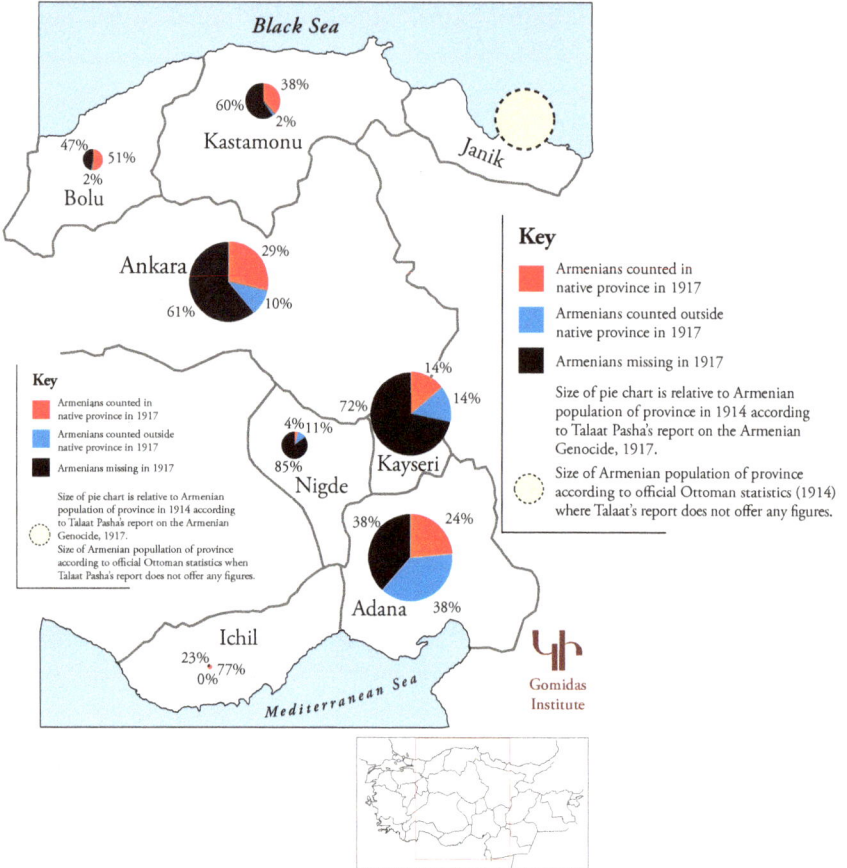

ANKARA (ANGORA) VILAYET[*]

Distribution of Ankara Armenians in 1917

Ankara (native)	12,766	

Adana	101	
Afyonkarahisar	578	
Aydin	219	
Beirut	50	
Bolu	9	
Eskishehir	62	
Aleppo	373	
Ichil	5	(from Yozgat)
Karesi	13	
Kastamonu	13	(from Yozgat)
Kayseri	87	
Konia	1,518	
Kutahya	2	
Mosul	52	
Nigde	1	
Sivas	31	(24 from Yozgat and 7 from Chorum)
Syria	1,234	
Urfa	142	
Izmit	13	
Zor	10	
TOTAL	4,513	17,280

Talaat Pasha's Summary Data

Native Armenians of vilayet (1914)	44,661	
Native Armenians in vilayet (1917)	12,766	
Native Armenians outside vilayet (1917)	4,560	
Missing native Armenian population (1917)	27,335	(-61%)

---

[*] Talaat's report gave the following figures for Armenians by place of origin in Ankara in 1917: Ankara (native) 12,766; Kayseri 257; Sivas 74; Eskishehir 20; Constantinople 18; Nigde 8, Elazig 6; Hudavendigar 5; Erzerum 5; Izmit 3; Van 3; Diyarbekir 3; Chankiri 3; Bitlis 2; Trebizond 1; Egypt 1; Caucasus 1. Total 13,176.

BOLU MUTASARRIFLIK[*]

Distribution of Bolu Armenians in 1917

Bolu (native)	1,539	
Aydin	8	
Kastamonu	3	
Syria	54	
Izmit	2	
TOTAL	67	1,606

Talaat Pasha's Summary Data

Native Armenians of vilayet (1914)	3,002	
Native Armenians in vilayet (1917)	1,539	
Native Armenians outside vilayet (1917)	67	
Missing native Armenian population (1917)	1,396	(-46%)

---

[*]   Talaat's report gave the following figures for Armenians by place of origin in Bolu in 1917: Bolu (native) 1,539; Izmit 155; Konia 155; Constantinople 48; Kastamonu 45; Elazig 37; Erzerum 28; Bursa 26; Trebizond 15; Van 10; Ankara 9; Sivas 9; Edirne 4; Kayseri 3; Bitlis 3; Janik 2; Adana 1; Beirut 1. Total 2,090.

KASTAMONU VILAYET[*]
Distribution of Kastamonu Armenians in 1917

Kastamonu (native)   3,437

Adana	61	
Ankara	3	(from Chankiri)
Aydin	9	
Bolu	45	
Aleppo	82	
Konia	3	
Sivas	2	
Urfa	17	
TOTAL	232	3,669

Talaat Pasha's Summary Data

Native Armenians of vilayet (1914)	9,052	
Native Armenians in vilayet (1917)	3,437	
Native Armenians outside vilayet (1917)	232	
Missing native Armenian population (1917)	5,383	(-60%)

---

[*] Talaat's report gave the following figures for Armenians by place of origin in Kastamonu in 1917: Kastamonu (native) 3,437; Trebizond 93; Sivas 33; Constantinople 21; Yozgat 13; Erzerum 6; Kala-i Sultaniye 5; Janik 4; Bolu 3; Kutahya 2; Elazig 2; Ayntap 2; Diyarbekir 1. Total 3,622.

JANIK MUTASARRIFLIK*
Distribution of Janik Armenians in 1917

Samsun	n/i
Bolu	2
Karesi	1
Sivas	128
Kastamonu	4
Aydin	21
Syria	7
Zor	9
Aleppo	6
TOTAL	178

Talaat Pasha's Summary Data

Native Armenians of vilayet (1914)	n/i	†
Native Armenians in vilayet (1917)	n/i	
Native Armenians outside vilayet (1917)	178	
Missing native Armenian population (1917)	n/i	‡

---

* There was no separate return for Janik in Talaat Pasha's report. The data presented here was gathered from the returns of the 23 other provinces that appeared in the report.

† According to official Ottoman population statistics for 1914, there were 27,319 Apostolic and Catholic Armenians in Janik. See T. C. Genelkurmay Başkanlığı, *Arşiv Belgeleriyle*, vol. 1, p. 643.

‡ According to Turkish militay archives all 26,374 Armenians in Janik mutasarriflik were deported to Zor and Mosul via Amasia, Karahisar and Sivas. *Arşiv Belgeleriyle*, vol. 1, p. 438 and 444.

NIGDE MUTASARRIFLIK[*]
Distribution of Nigde Armenians in 1917

Nigde (native)	193	
Ankara	8	
Aydin	7	
Beirut	15	
Aleppo	167	
Ichil	7	
Konia	5	
Syria	131	
Urfa	214	
Zor	1	
TOTAL	555	748

Talaat Pasha's Summary Data

Native Armenians of vilayet (1914)	4,939	
Native Armenians in vilayet (1917)	193	
Native Armenians outside vilayet (1917)	555	
Missing native Armenian population (1917)	4,191	(-85%)

---

[*] Talaat's report gave the following figures for Armenians by place of origin in Nigde in 1917: Nigde (native) 193; Izmit 776; Karesi 20; Kayseri 17; Sivas 10; Edirne 8; Konia 6; Erzerum 5; Elazig 5; Ankara 1; Eskishehir 1; Adana 1. Total 1,043.

KAYSERI MUTASARRIFLIK[*]

Distribution of Kayseri Armenians in 1917

Kayseri (native)	6,650	
Adana	539	
Afyonkarahisar		
Ankara	257	
Aydin	1,600	
Beirut	39	
Bolu	3	
Eskishehir	8	
Aleppo	838	
Ichil	40	
Karesi	1	
Konia	16	
Kutahya		
Mosul	182	
Nigde	17	
Sivas	113	
Syria	2,683	
Urfa	580	
Izmit	14	
Zor	49	
TOTAL	6,979	13,629

Talaat Pasha's Summary Data

Native Armenians of vilayet (1914)	47,974	
Native Armenians in vilayet (1917)	6,650	
Native Armenians outside vilayet (1917)	6,979	
Missing native Armenian population (1917)	34,345	(-71%)

---

[*] Talaat's report gave the following figures for Armenians by place of origin in Kayseri in 1917: Kayseri (native) 6,650; Ankara 87; Sivas 21; Constantinople 3. Total 6,761.

ADANA VILAYET[*]

Distribution of Adana Armenians in 1917

Adana (native)	12,263	
Aydin	78	
Beirut	667	
Bolu	1	
Aleppo	4,757	
Ichil	40	
Karesi	1	
Konia	1	
Mosul	1,074	
Nigde	1	
Syria	11,273	
Urfa	1,461	
Zor	312	
TOTAL	19,666	31,929

Talaat Pasha's Summary Data

Native Armenians of vilayet (1914)	51,723	
Native Armenians in vilayet (1917)	12,263	
Native Armenians outside vilayet (1917)	19,666	
Missing native Armenian population (1917)	19,797	(-38%)

---

[*] Talaat's report gave the following figures for Armenians by place of origin by place of origin in Adana in 1917: Adana (native) 12,263; Taurus construction zone1,152; Aleppo 682; Kayseri 539; Marash 344; Elazig 303; Konia 207; Diyarbekir 144; Hudavendigar 131; Sivas 116; Ankara 101; Edirne 95; Izmit 82; Constantinople 72; Kastamonu 61; Urfa 56; Bitlis 42; Aydin 41; Erzerum 30; Karesi 22; Van 20; Ichil 17. Total 16,520.

ICHIL MUTASARRIFLIK[*]
Distribution of Ichil Armenians in 1917

Ichil (native)	252	
Adana	17	
TOTAL	17	269

Talaat Pasha's Summary Data

Native Armenians of vilayet (1914)	350	
Native Armenians in vilayet (1917)	252	
Native Armenians outside vilayet (1917)	17	
Missing native Armenian population (1917)	81	(-23%)

---

[*] Talaat's report gave the following figures for Armenians by place of origin in 1917: Ichil (native) 252; Kayseri 40; Adana 40; Konia 15; Nigde 7; Aydin 6; Yozgat 5; Sivas 3. Total 368.

APPENDED

EASTERN PROVINCES

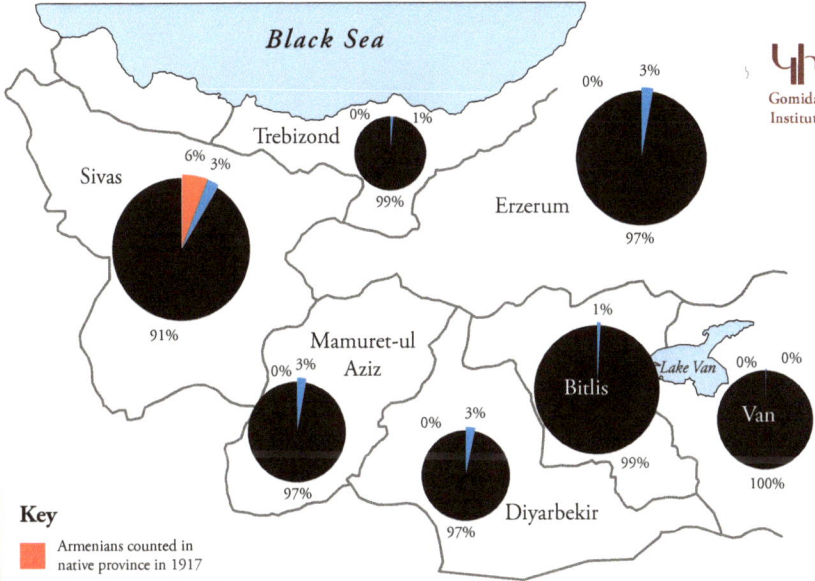

Black Sea

Trebizond
0%   1%
99%

Sivas
6% 3%
91%

Erzerum
0%   3%
97%

Mamuret-ul Aziz
0% 3%
97%

Diyarbekir
0%   3%
97%

Bitlis
1%
99%

Lake Van

Van
0% 0%
100%

Key

Armenians counted in
native province in 1917

Armenians counted outside
native province in 1917

Armenians missing in 1917

Size of pie chart is relative to Armenian
population of province in 1914 according
to Talaat Pasha's report on the Armenian
Genocide, 1917.

Size of Armenian population of province
according to official Ottoman statistics when
Talaat Pasha's report does not offer any figures.

Gomidas
Institute

APPENDED

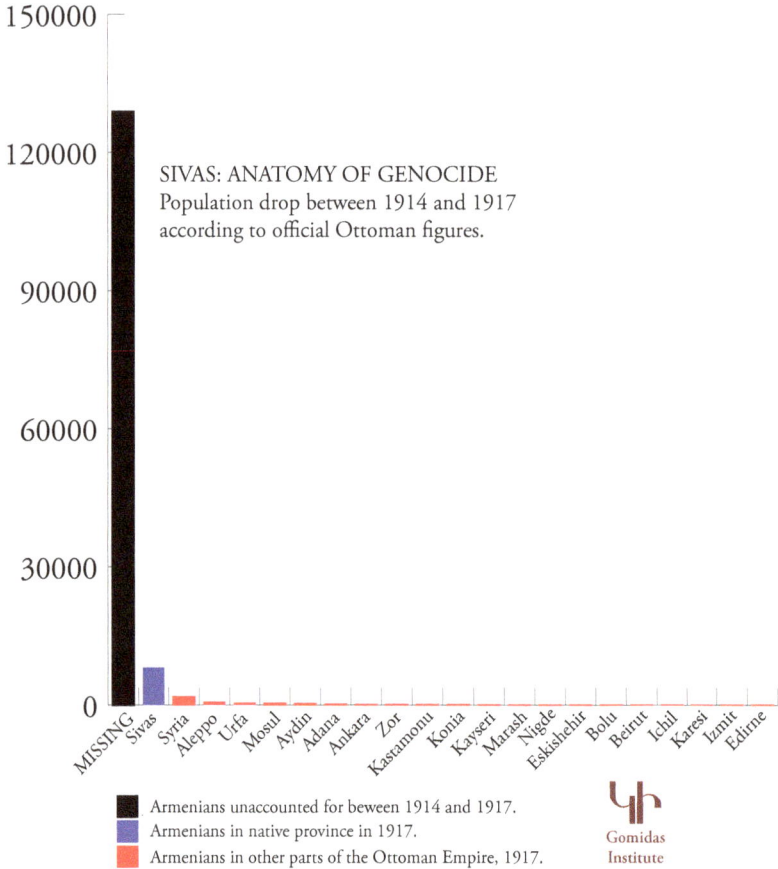

SIVAS: ANATOMY OF GENOCIDE
Population drop between 1914 and 1917
according to official Ottoman figures.

Legend:
- Armenians unaccounted for beween 1914 and 1917.
- Armenians in native province in 1917.
- Armenians in other parts of the Ottoman Empire, 1917.

Gomidas
Institute

Sivas was the most populous Armenian inhabited province of the Ottoman Empire on the eve of WWI. However, by the beginning of 1917, most Armenians from Sivas had disappeared in the previous three years.

SIVAS VILAYET[*]

Distribution of Sivas Armenians in 1917

Sivas (native)	8,097	
Adana	116	
Ankara	74	
Aydin	303	
Beirut	5	
Bolu	9	
Edirne	1	
Eskishehir	9	
Aleppo	681	
Ichil	3	
Izmit	1	
Karesi	2	
Kastamonu	33	
Kayseri	21	
Konia	30	
Marash	13	from Amasia
Mosul	364	
Nigde	10	
Syria	1,744	
Urfa	509	
Zor	46	
TOTAL	3,974	12,122

Talaat Pasha's Summary Data

Native Armenians of vilayet (1914)	141,000	
Native Armenians in vilayet (1917)	8,097	
Native Armenians outside vilayet (1917)	4,025	
Missing native Armenian population (1917)	128,878	(-91%)

---

[*] Talaat's report gave the following figures for Armenians by place of origin in Sivas in 1917: Sivas (native) 8,097; Trebizond 364; Erzerum 235; Janik 128; Kayseri 113; Elazig 63; Yozgat 24; Chorum 7; Constantinople 5; Salonika 3; Kastamonu 2; Konia 1; Aydin 1; Diyarbekir 1; Edirne 1. Total 9,045.

ERZERUM VILAYET
Distribution of Erzerum Armenians in 1917

Erzerum (native)	0
Adana	30
Ankara	5
Aydin	481
Beirut	4
Bolu	28
Aleppo	257
Karesi	11
Kastamonu	6
Marash	163
Mosul	901
Nigde	5
Sivas	235
Syria	761
Urfa	443
Zor	34
TOTAL	3,364

Talaat Pasha's Summary Data

Native Armenians of vilayet (1914)	125,657	
Native Armenians in vilayet (1917)	0	
Native Armenians outside vilayet (1917)	3,364	
Missing native Armenian population (1917)	122,293	(-97%)

BITLIS VILAYET
Distribution of Bitlis Armenians in 1917

Bitlis (native)	0
Adana	42
Ankara	2
Aydin	294
Beirut	1
Bolu	3
Eskishehir	21
Aleppo	216
Izmit	22
Karesi	1
Konia	3
Mosul	431
Syria	24
Zor	1
TOTAL	1,061

Talaat Pasha's Summary Data

Native Armenians of vilayet (1914)	114,704	
Native Armenians in vilayet (1917)	0	
Native Armenians outside vilayet (1917)	1,061	
Missing native Armenian population (1917)	113,643	(-99)

VAN VILAYET
Distribution of Van Armenians in 1917

Van (native)	0	
Adana	20	
Ankara	3	
Aydin	74	
Bolu	10	
Izmit	24	
Karesi	28	
Konia	1	
Mosul	87	(from Hakkiari)
TOTAL	247	

Talaat Pasha's Summary Data

Native Armenians of vilayet (1914)	67,792	
Native Armenians in vilayet (1917)	0	
Native Armenians outside vilayet (1917)	247	
Missing native Armenian population (1917)	67,545	(-99%)

TREBIZOND VILAYET
Distribution of Trebizond Armenians in 1917

Trebizond (native)	0
Ankara	1
Aydin	46
Bolu	15
Izmit	1
Kastamonu	93
Konia	2
Mosul	18
Sivas	364
Syria	40
TOTAL	580

Talaat Pasha's Summary Data

Native Armenians of vilayet (1914)	37,549	
Native Armenians in vilayet (1917)	0	
Native Armenians outside vilayet (1917)	580	
Missing native Armenian population (1917)	36,969	(-98)

MAMURET-UL-AZIZ (ELAZIG) VILAYET
Distribution of Elazig Armenians in 1917

Elazig (native)	0	
Adana	303	
Ankara	6	
Aydin	254	
Beirut	63	
Bolu	37	
Aleppo	606	
Izmit	2	
Karesi	2	(from Malatya)
Kastamonu	2	
Konia	1	
Marash	2	
Mosul	112	
Nigde	5	
Sivas	63	
Syria	585	
Urfa	84	
Zor	76	
TOTAL	2,203	

Talaat Pasha's Summary Data

Native Armenians of vilayet (1914)	70,060	
Native Armenians in vilayet (1917)	0	
Native Armenians outside vilayet (1917)	2,203	
Missing native Armenian population (1917)	67,857	(-97%)

APPENDED

SOUTH-EASTERN PROVINCES AND RESETTLEMENT ZONE

Gomidas Institute

Key

- Armenians counted in native province in 1917
- Armenians counted outside native province in 1917
- Armenians missing in 1917

Size of pie chart is relative to Armenian population of province in 1914 according to Talaat Pasha's report on the Armenian Genocide, 1917.

Size of Armenian population of province according to official Ottoman statistics when Talaat's report does not offer any figures.

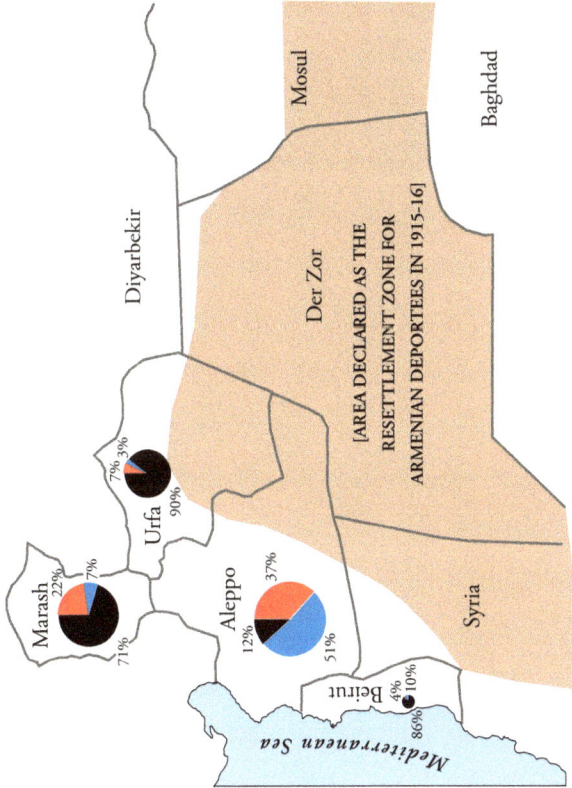

Mosul

Baghdad

Diyarbekir

Der Zor

[AREA DECLARED AS THE RESETTLEMENT ZONE FOR ARMENIAN DEPORTEES IN 1915-16]

Syria

Urfa
7% 3%
90%

Marash
22% 7%
71%

Aleppo
12% 37%
51%

Beirut
4% 10%
86%

Mediterranean Sea

MARASH MUTASARRIFLIK[*]

Distribution of Marash Armenians in 1917

Marash (native)	6,115	
Adana	344	
Aydin	50	
Beirut	213	
Mosul	435	
Urfa	715	
Zor	353	
TOTAL	2,110	8,225

Talaat Pasha's Summary Data

Native Armenians of vilayet (1914)	27,306	
Native Armenians in vilayet (1917)	6,115	
Native Armenians outside vilayet (1917)	2,110	
Missing native Armenian population (1917)	19,081	(-70%)

---

[*] Talaat's report gave the following figures for Armenians by place of origin in Marash in 1917: Marash (native) 6,115; Erzerum 163; Amasia 20; Sivas 13; Elazig 2. Total 6,313.

ALEPPO (HALEP) VILAYET[*]
Distribution of Aleppo Armenians in 1917

Aleppo (native)	13,679	
Adana	682	
Aydin	46	
Beirut	370	
Kastamonu	2	(from Ayntap)
Konia	1	
Mosul	847	
Syria	16,018	
Urfa	901	
Zor	227	
TOTAL	19,094	32,773

Talaat Pasha's Summary Data

Native Armenians of vilayet (1914)	37,031	
Native Armenians in vilayet (1917)	13,679	
Native Armenians outside vilayet (1917)	19,094	
Missing native Armenian population (1917)	4,258	(-11%)

---

[*] Talaat's report gave the following figures for Armenians in Aleppo in 1917: Aleppo (native) 13,679; Adana 4,757; Izmit 862; Kayseri 838; Diyarbekir 796; Sivas 681; Elazig 606; Konia 469; Ankara 373; Erzerum 257; Bitlis 216; Hudavendigar 192; Nigde 167; Eskishehir 129; Karesi 83; Kastamonu 82; Constantinople 73; Afyon Karahissar 52; Aydin 34; Syria 30; Janik 6. Total 24,382.

URFA MUTASARRIFLIK[*]
Distribution of Urfa Armenians in 1917

Urfa (native)	1,144	
Adana	56	
Aydin	29	
Beirut	5	
Mosul	191	
Syria	129	
Zor	41	
TOTAL	451	1,595

Talaat Pasha's Summary Data

Native Armenians of vilayet (1914)	15,616	
Native Armenians in vilayet (1917)	1,144	
Native Armenians outside vilayet (1917)	451	
Missing native Armenian population (1917)	14,021	(-90%)

---

[*]   Talaat's report gave the following figures for Armenians by place of origin in Urfa in 1917: Urfa (native) 1,144; Adana 1,461; Aleppo 901; Marash 715; Kayseri 580; Sivas 509; Erzerum 443; Konia 311; Izmit 309; Hudavendigar 285; Karesi 244; Nigde 214; Eskishehir 188; Ankara 142; Edirne 133; Afyon Karahissar 111; Elazig 84; Diyarbekir 35; Kastamonu 17; Constantinople 5. Total 7,831.

DIYARBEKIR VILAYET

Distribution of Diyarbekir Armenians in 1917

Dıyarbekir (native)	0
Adana	144
Ankara	3
Aydin	73
Beirut	177
Aleppo	796
Kastamonu	1
Sivas	1
Syria	598
Urfa	35
Zor	21
TOTAL	1,849

Talaat Pasha's Summary Data

Native Armenians of vilayet (1914)	56,166	
Native Armenians in vilayet (1917)	n/i	
Native Armenians outside vilayet (1917)	1,849	
Missing native Armenian population (1917)	54,317	(-97%)

APPENDED

Comidas
Institute

ARMENIANS IN SYRIA, 1917
ACCORDING TO THEIR PLACES OF ORIGIN

The following pie charts show the main concentrations of Armenians in Syria as reported in the 1917 population survey of Ottoman Armenians. These figures were tabulated and appear in a more concise form in *Talaat Pasha's Report on the Armenian Genocide*. The total number of Armenians reported in Syria was 39,409. These five regions represent 35,837 of them. The majority of these survivors were from Adana and Aleppo provinces.

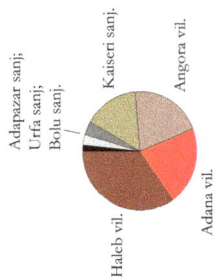

KERAK SANJAK
6,173

Mamuretulaziz vil;
Bidis vil.

Diyarbekir vil.
Sivas vil.

Kaiseri sanj.

Adana viayet

Haleb vil.

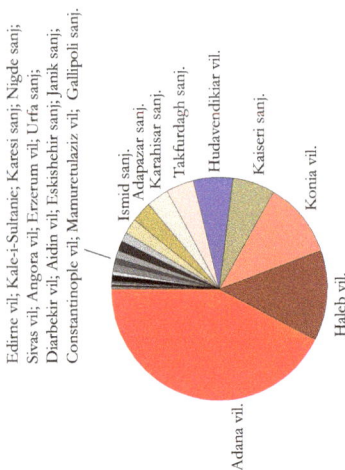

DAMASCUS CENTRE
9,670

Edirne vil; Kale-i-Sultanie; Karesi sanj; Nigde sanj;
Sivas vil; Angora vil; Erzerum vil; Urfa sanj;
Diarbekir vil; Aidin vil; Eskisßehir sanj; Janik sanj;
Constantinople vil; Mamuretulaziz vil; Gallipoli sanj.

Ismid sanj.
Adapazar sanj.
Karahisar sanj.
Takfurdagh sanj.
Hudavendikiar vil.
Kaiseri sanj.
Konia vil.
Haleb vil.
Adana vil.

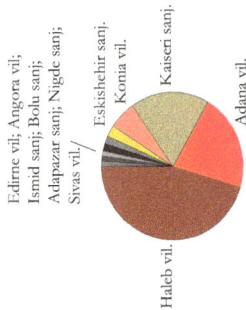

ERZIT/AZRA
1,737

Adapazar sanj;
Urfa sanj;
Bolu sanj.

Kaiseri sanj.

Angora vil.

Adana vil.

Haleb vil.

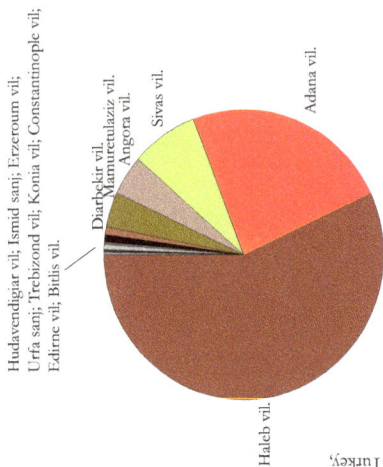

HAMA CENTRE
15,028

Hudavendigiar vil; Ismid sanj; Erzeroum vil;
Urfa sanj; Trebizond vil; Konia vil; Constantinople vil;
Edirne vil; Bidis vil.

Diarbekir vil.
Mamuretulaziz vil.
Angora vil.
Sivas vil.
Adana vil.

Haleb vil.

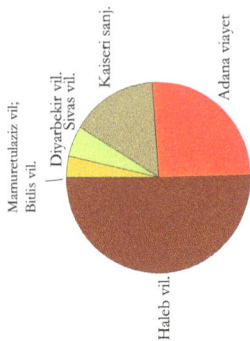

AJLOUN KAZA
3,279

Edirne vil; Angora vil;
Ismid sanj; Bolu sanj;
Adapazar sanj; Nigde sanj;
Sivas vil.

Eskisßehir sanj.
Konia vil.
Kaiseri sanj.

Adana vil.

Haleb vil.

SYRIA VILAYET[*]
Distribution of Syria Armenians in 1917

Syria (native)   0 [†]

Talaat Pasha's Summary Data
Native Armenians of vilayet (1914)   0
Native Armenians in vilayet (1917)   0
Native Armenians outside vilayet (1917)   0
Missing native Armenian population (1917)   0

[NOTE: While the Ottoman province of Syria did not have a native Armenian population on the eve of WWI, this region became a major deportation destination in 1915-16. Despite horrific conditions, a large number of deportees managed to survive in this region under the protection of Jemal Pasha. There were no massacres in Syria.]

---

[*] Talaat's report gave the following figures for Armenians by place of origin in Syria in 1917: Syria (native) 0; Aleppo 16,018; Adana 11,273; Kayseri 2,683; Sivas 1,744; Konia 1,525; Ankara 1,234; Izmit 797; Erzerum 761; Hudavendigar 726; Edirne 677; Diyarbekir 598; Elazig 585; Afyon Karahissar 419; Nigde 131; Urfa 129; Kala-i Sultaniye 129; Karesi 128; Eskishehir 113; Bolu 54; Trebizond 40; Bitlis 24; Aydin 21; Constantinople 13; Jerusalem 8; Janik 7. Total 39,837.

[†] According to official Ottoman population statistics for 1914, there were 406 Apostolic and 241 Catholic Armenians in Syria. Protestant Armenians were not counted separately and have been left out of our calculations. See *Arşiv Belgeleriyle*, p. 627.

ZOR MUTASARRIFLIK[*]
Distribution of Zor Armenians in 1917

Zor (native)   201

Talaat Pasha's Summary Data
Native Armenians of vilayet (1914)   63   [†]
Native Armenians in vilayet (1917)   201
Native Armenians outside vilayet (1917)   0
Missing native Armenian population (1917)   0

[NOTE: The Der Zor returns in the 1917 population survey of Armenians reported 1,771 Armenians in this region. These figures were scrutinized by Ottoman authorities and increased to 6,778 in a footnote appearing in Talaat Pasha's report on the Armenian Genocide. The footnote does not give a detailed breakdown of its revised figures. These files related to Der Zor and the 1917 population survey have not been released by the Prime Ministry State Archives in Turkey.]

---

* Talaat's report gave the following figures for Armenians by place of origin in Zor in 1917: Zor (native) 201; Marash 353; Adana 312; Aleppo 227; Hudavendigar 130; Izmit 85; Elazig 76; Kayseri 49; Konia 48; Sivas 46; Urfa 41; Edirne 38; Erzerum 34; Karesi 22; Diyarbekir 21; Constantinople 20; Afyon Karahissar 19; Ankara 10; Aydin 10; Beirut 9; Janik 9; Eskishehir 5; Kala-i Sultaniye 4; Nigde 1; Bitlis 1. Total 1,771. Note: Talaat's 1917 data changes the total number of outsiders to 6,778 people (without giving a new breakdown of the figures). This alternative number was used in the report's summary analysis.

† According to official Ottoman population statistics for 1914, the Armenian population of Zor mutasarriflik was 67 Apostolic Armenians and 215 Catholic Armenian. The number of Protestant Armenians was not recorded separately. See *Arşiv Belgeleriyle*, p. 653.

APPENDED

Gomidas
Institute

— 300,000 deportees

DER ZOR: THE MISSING ARCHIVAL
RECORDS IN TURKEY*

**300,000 to 600,000 Armenians
deported to Der Zor, 1915-16
(conservative estimates)**

— 6,778 (amended figures in
Talaat's personal report)
— 1,771 (original 1917 survey
results)

Der Zor was the final destination of hundreds of thousand of Armenian deportees in 1915-16. According to US Consul Jesse B. Jackson in Aleppo, most deportees were killed during the deportations, but 300,000 reached Der Zor by Feb. 1916, and more followed. Practically none of the deportees survived in Der Zor, as they were wasted away and massacred in the summer of 1916. See Jesse B. Jackson to Ambassador Morgenthau dated Aleppo, 8 Feb. 1916, and August Bernau's report in Jesse B. Jackson to Philippe Hoffman, Charge d'Affaires (Constantinople) dated Aleppo, 21 Sept. 1916 in *United States Official Records on the Armenian Genocide, 1915-16*, comp. and ed. Ara Sarafian, (London: Gomidas Institute, 2019), pp. 489-90, and 553-560.

* The actual Der Zor returns in the 1917 population survey of Armenians and other records related to Der Zor in *Talaat Pasha's Report on the Armenian Genocide* have not been made available to researchers at the Prime Ministry Ottoman State Archives in Turkey. The critical summaries of the figures on the facing page, found in Talaat Pasha's possession, are thus of particular significance.

MOSUL VILAYET[*]
Distribution of Mosul Armenians in 1917

Mosul (native)   253

Talaat Pasha's Summary Data
Native Armenians of vilayet (1914)   0 [†]
Native Armenians in vilayet (1917)   253
Native Armenians outside vilayet (1917)   0
Missing native Armenian population (1917)   n/i

---

[*] Talaat's report gave the following figures for Armenians by place of origin in Mosul in 1917: Mosul (native) 253; Adana 1,074; Hudavendigar 1,012; Erzerum 901; Aleppo 847; Izmit 607; Marash 435; Bitlis 431; Konia 407; Sivas 364; Urfa 191; Kayseri 182; Ankara 152; Elazig 112; Beirut 106; Hakkari 87; Rodosto 60; Eskishehir 30; Trebizond 18; Constantinople 9. Total 7,278.

[†] Official Ottoman population statistics for 1914 do not give figures for Mosul. See *Arşiv Belgeleriyle*. However, the 1906/7 census, which only gave figures for men, counted 45 Apostolic and 4,726 Catholic Armenians. See Kemal Karpat, *Ottoman Population 1830-1914: Demographic and Social Characteristics,* Madison: The University of Wisconsin Press, 1985, p. 166.

BEIRUT VILAYET[*]
Distribution of Beirut Armenians in 1917

Beirut (native)	50	
Aydin	6	
Bolu	1	
Mosul	106	
Zor	9	
TOTAL	122	172

Talaat Pasha's Summary Data

Native Armenians of vilayet (1914)	1,224	
Native Armenians in vilayet (1917)	50	
Native Armenians outside vilayet (1917)	122	
Missing native Armenian population (1917)	1,052	(-86%)

---

[*] Talaat's report gave the following figures for Armenians by place of origin in Beirut in 1917: Beirut (native) 50; Adana 667; Aleppo 370; Marash 213; Diyarbekir 177; Konia 83; Elazig 63; Constantinople 54; Ankara 50; Kayseri 39; Izmit 22; Afyon Karahissar 17; Jerusalem 16; Nigde 15; Hudavendigar 14; Karesi 9; Varna 7; Edirne 6; Sivas 5; Urfa 5; Eskishehir 4; Erzerum 4; Filibe 4; Syria 2; Bitlis 1; Dedeaghach 1; Tiflis 1. Total 1,899.

JERUSALEM (KUDUS-I SHERIF) VILAYET[*]
Distribution of native Armenians of province, 1917

Jerusalem	n/i
Beirut	16

Talaat Pasha's Summary Data

Native Armenians of vilayet (1914)	n/i [†]
Native Armenians in vilayet (1917)	n/i
Native Armenians outside vilayet (1917)	16
Missing native Armenian population (1917)	n/i

---

[*] There was no return for Kudus-i Serif (Jerusalem) in Talaat Pasha's report. The data presented here was gathered from the returns of the 23 other provinces that appeared in the report.

[†] According to official Ottoman figures for 1914, there were 1,310 Apostolic Armenians in Jerusalem. See *Arşiv Belgeleriyle*, p. 653.

APPENDIXES

Appendix 1

A Report from the Turkish Military Archives

The following Ottoman document from the Turkish military archives was published by the Turkish General Staff in Ankara.[*] It shows the number of Armenians who were liable for deportation in 1915, the number who were deported, the route taken by deportees along with their destination, and the fate of those who were not deported.

The deportation records are not complete for all areas, though they still account for the expulsion of over half a million Ottoman Armenians.

The authorship and date of the document are not mentioned, nor is its provenance discussed by the publishers of the report. However, the population data that is presented for Ottoman Armenians in 1914 are practically identical to those presented in another Ottoman document in Talaat Pasha's possession, the so-called "black booklet," also published by Murat Bardakçı (See Appendix 2).

For all its limitations, this document shows that all Armenians were slated for deportation, the number of Armenians who escaped from the border regions of Erzerum and Trebizond was small, deportations were enforced in a comprehensive manner [except in Bitlis where there were massacres or people escaped], and the official destination of deportees was mainly Der Zor and Mosul. The absence of information on Van is probably due to the fact that Armenians in several parts of the province mounted successful resistance against Ottoman forces and many were eventually saved by the Russian army.

Needless to say, this table reflects the official Turkish denial of the Armenian Genocide, in this case by the historical section of the Turkish army, in its assertion that there were fewer than a million Armenians in the Ottoman Empire on the eve of World War One, and that they were mostly 'transferred' and 'resettled' in the lower Euphrates between 1915-16. The center for their resettlement was Der Zor and surrounding areas.

---

[*] See facsimile of the original report as well as a modern Turkish transliteration in T. C. Genelkurmay Başkanlığı, *Arşiv Belgeleriyle Ermeni Faaliyetleri, 1914-1918*, Ankara: Genelkurmay Basım Evi, 2005, vol. 1, pp. 439-456.

Despatch and Resettlement of Armenians by Vilayet [province] and Sanjak [sub-province]

Province	Registered population	Deported	Destination	Note
Ankara Vilayet	47,224	n/i		
Erzerum Vilayet	128,657	120,000	Zor Sanjak	Killed in clashes or escaped
Adana Vilayet	46,031	n/i		
Izmit Sanjak	54,370	50,000	Zor Sanjak	Escaped, went into hiding, or killed
Eskishehir Sanjak	n/i	n/i		
Bitlis Vilayet	109,521	20,000	Diyarbekir via Siirt and Zor and Mosul via Mamuretulaziz	Killed in clashes and or escaped
Janik Sanjak	26,374	26,374	Zor and Mosul via Amasya and Karahisar	
Aleppo Vilayet	34,451	n/i		
Hudavendigar Vilayet	66,413	n/i		
Diyarbekir Vilayet	61,002	n/i		
Sivas Vilayet	141,592	141,592	Zor and Mosul via Malatya	
Trebizond Vilayet	34,500	28,000	Zor and Mosul via Gumushhane	Killed in clashes
Karesi Sanjak	8,290	n/i		
Karahisar Sanjak	7,327	n/i		
Kayseri Sanjak	47,617	n/i		
Mamuretulaziz Vilayet	74,206	n/i		
Marash Sanjak	27,101	27,101	Sent to Zor and Syria via Aleppo	

DESPATCH AND RESETTLEMENT OF ARMENIANS BY VILAYET AND SANJAK

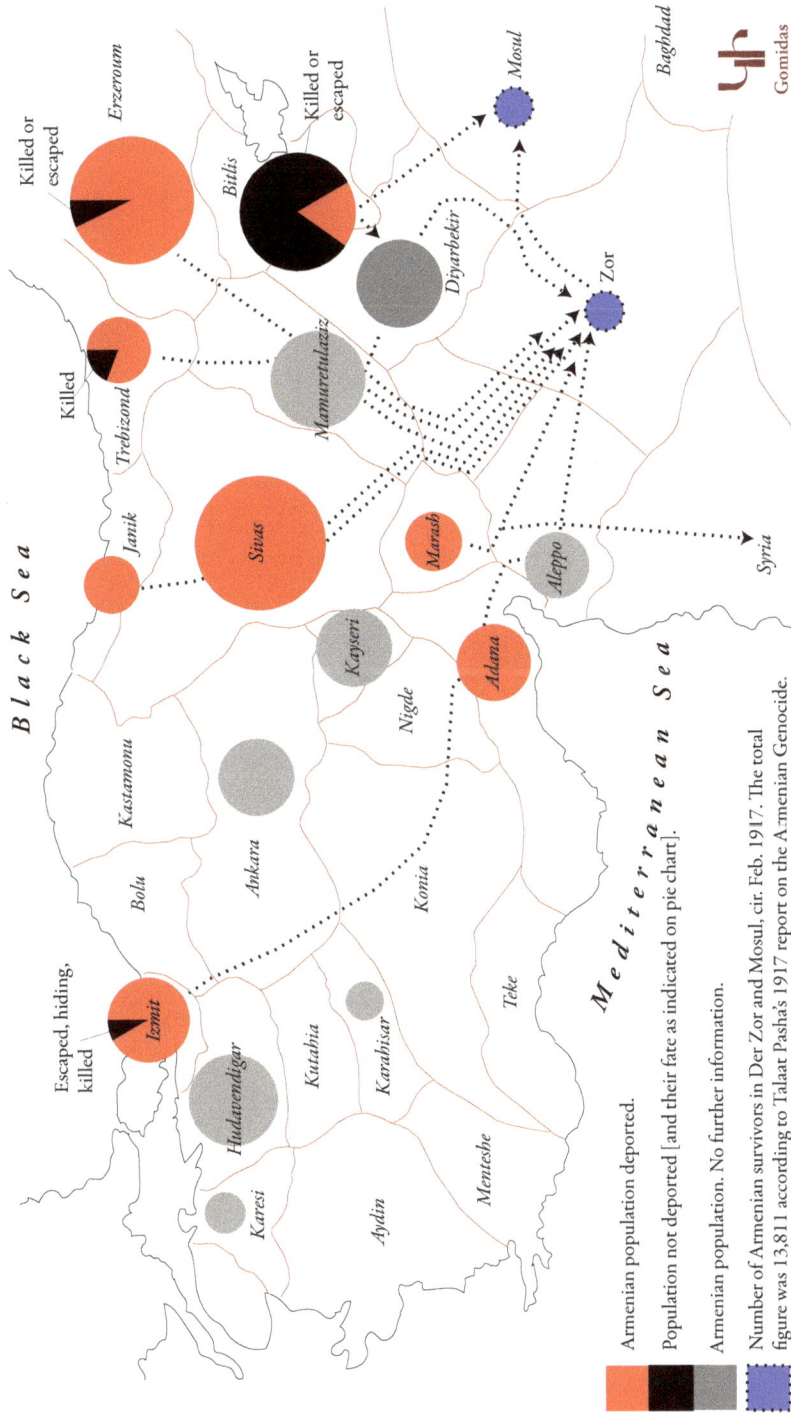

SOURCE: T. C. Genelkurmay Başkanlığı, *Arşiv Belgeleriyle Ermeni Faaliyetleri, 1914-1918*, Ankara: Genelkurmay Basım Evi, 2005, vol. 1, pp. 439-456.

Appendix 2

Talaat Pasha's Black Book

A second document from Talaat Pasha's private papers published by Murat Bardakçı is a 66 page, handwritten, untitled booklet with a black cover. It is composed of statistics, charts, and color maps.[*] The booklet's internal evidence suggests that it was prepared sometime after late 1916. It was almost certainly commissioned by Talaat Pasha.

The focus of this "black book" is the demographic engineering of a shrinking Ottoman Empire between 1877 and 1916 with the careful settlement of Muslim emigrants and refugees in government held areas, as well as the systematic liquidation of Christian communities, most notably Armenians.

The destruction of Armenians and the confiscation of their properties is presented within the context of the so-called "despatch" (*sevk*) of Armenians and the management of their "abandoned" properties left behind. Starting with a table showing "The Number of Armenians who Were Sent Away," the focus of this table is the removal of Armenians, with a list of 18 vilayets and sanjaks and their Armenian populations.[†] The total number of Armenians is given as 924,158, a figure that reflects the number of Apostolic (or Gregorian) Armenians in these provinces according to official Ottoman statistics for 1914.[‡] The list does not include the European provinces of the Ottoman Empire, nor Kutahya or

---

[*] See Murat Bardakçı, *Talat Paşa'nın Evrak-ı Metrukesi : Sadrazam Talat Paşa'nın özel arşivinde bulunan Ermeni tehciri konusundaki belgeler ve hususi yazışmalar* [The Remaining Documents of Talaat Pasha: Documents and Important Correspondence Found in the Private Archives of Sadrazam Talaat Pasha About the Transfer of Armenians], Istanbul: Everest Yayinlari, 2008, pp. 27-103.

[†] For full figures see Bardakçı, pp. 76-77.

[‡] This list confirms that all Armenians were slated for deportation, and the exclusion of Van and Kutahya on the list also confirms that there were no deportations in Van because of Armenian resistance and no deportations in Kutahya because of local (Muslim) opposition to the central government's plans.

Van.[*] It also does not mention the removal of Catholic and Protestant Armenians.[†] There are no corresponding tables of where these Armenians ended up or how they were compensated for resettlement purposes.

NUMBER OF ARMENIANS WHO WERE SENT AWAY

Ankara Vilayet 47,224; Erzerum Vilayet 128,657; Adana Vilayet 46,031; Bitlis Vilayet 109,521; Aleppo Vilayet 34,451; Hudavendigar Vilayet 66,451; Diyarbekir Vilayet 61,002; Sivas Vilayet 141,592; Trebizond Vilayet 34,500; Mamuretulaziz Vilayet 74,206; Izmit Sanjak 54,370; Janik Sanjak 26,374; Karesi Sanjak 8,290; Karahisar Sanjak 7,327; Kayseri Sanjak 47,617; Marash Sanjak 27,101; Nigde Sanjak 5,101; Konia Sanjak 4,381. Total 924,158[‡]

Regarding the Armenians who were sent away, their destination is simply marked on a map entitled "Areas Emptied and Resettled by Armenians." This zone corresponds to the official resettlement zone outlined by other Ottoman sources. This resettlement zone centers on the desert sub-province (sanjak) of Der Zor and includes the mostly inhospitable parts of Aleppo, Urfa, Syria and Mosul provinces.[**] The map clearly indicated that this is the location where 924,158 Armenians were sent. As we see in Talaat Pasha's Report on the Armenian Genocide, most Armenian deportees disappeared between 1915 and 1917, and their fate can be

---

[*] While the booklet does not mention the deportation of Armenians from the European provinces, it does mention the confiscation of 3,133 abandoned Armenian homes in Edirne vilayet.

[†] Bardakçı, p. 90-91.

[‡] See Bardakçı, pp. 76-77. A comparable dataset to the one appearing in the black booklet was also published by the Historical Section of the Turkish General Staff (ATASE) in Ankara. See *Arşiv Belgeleriyle Ermeni Faaliyetleri*, volume 1, pp. 439-56. This second document appears as Appendix I in the present work. According to Murat Bardakçı and Yusuf Halaçoğlu, both the black booklet and the document published by ATASE were from the same source. However, the second document gave additional details for seven regions where deportations had taken place (i.e., Erzerum, Izmit, Bitlis, Janik, Sivas, Trebizond and Marash). Of the 522,115 Armenians in these provinces in 1914, 413,067 (or 80 percent) were listed as actually "deported" to the official resettlement zone around Der Zor. The balance, that is, those not listed as having been deported from these provinces, are accounted for in terms of "killed in clashes," "escaped," or "went into hiding." One may thus conclude that all Armenians were liable for deportation, though not all were actually sent away as planned.

[**] Bardakçı, pp. 82–83.

discerned from eyewitness accounts of survivors and onlookers. There were practically no Armenians left at the very epicenter of the resettlement zone of Der Zor.

The booklet also indicates Talaat's interest in assimilating Armenians into Muslim communities with some details on Armenian orphans in the hands of Muslim and foreign institutions (6,768 and 3,501 respectively).[*] Forced assimilation and absorption of Armenian women and children into Muslim families was an integral part of the genocidal process.

The appropriation of Armenian (and Greek) properties, productive lands and mining concerns also figure prominently into Talaat's ledger, with the liquidation of Christian communities in favor of Muslim beneficiaries. Most of these properties are characterized as "abandoned properties" but some are described as "confiscated properties."

In a table entitled "The Number of Abandoned Empty Armenian Houses," the booklet records 40,717 properties seized from Armenians of Edirne, Adana, Ankara, Hudavendigar, Diyarbekir, Sivas, Mamuretulaziz, Konia, Urfa, Izmit, Eskishehir, Janik, Karesi, Kayseri, Nigde, and Marash.[†] This table does not mention any properties confiscated in Erzerum, Trebizond, Van and Bitlis, possibly because they were either under Russian occupation or close to war zones.

NUMBER OF ABANDONED EMPTY ARMENIAN HOUSES[‡]

Edirne Vilayet 3,133; Adana Vilayet 699; Ankara Vilayet 2,540; Hudavendigar Vilayet 14,856; Diyarbekir Vilayet 1,055; Sivas Vilayet 3,000; Mamuretulaziz Vilayet 3,500; Konia Vilayet 270; Urfa Vilayet 250; Izmit Vilayet 3,589; Eskishehir Vilayet [no data]; Janik Vilayet 614; Karesi Vilayet 2,870; Kayseri Vilayet 3,000; Karahissar-i Sahib Vilayet [no data]; Nigde Sanjak 341; Marash Sanjak 1,000. Total 40,717.

---

[*] See Bardakçı, pp. 88-89. Some additional information was also given about the "other" category in footnotes: The American Girls' College, 400 girls, and 15 children in Haruniye; 530 children in Aleppo vilayet were under the care of two German women with Jemal Pasha's permission; and 70 children in the Armenian orphanage in Sivas.

[†] Bardakçı, pp. 90-93.

[‡] Bardakçı, pp. 90-91. Note: Eskishehir, Janik, Karesi, Kayseri, Karahissar-i Sahib (Shabinkarahissar) should not be vilayets but mutasarrifliks.

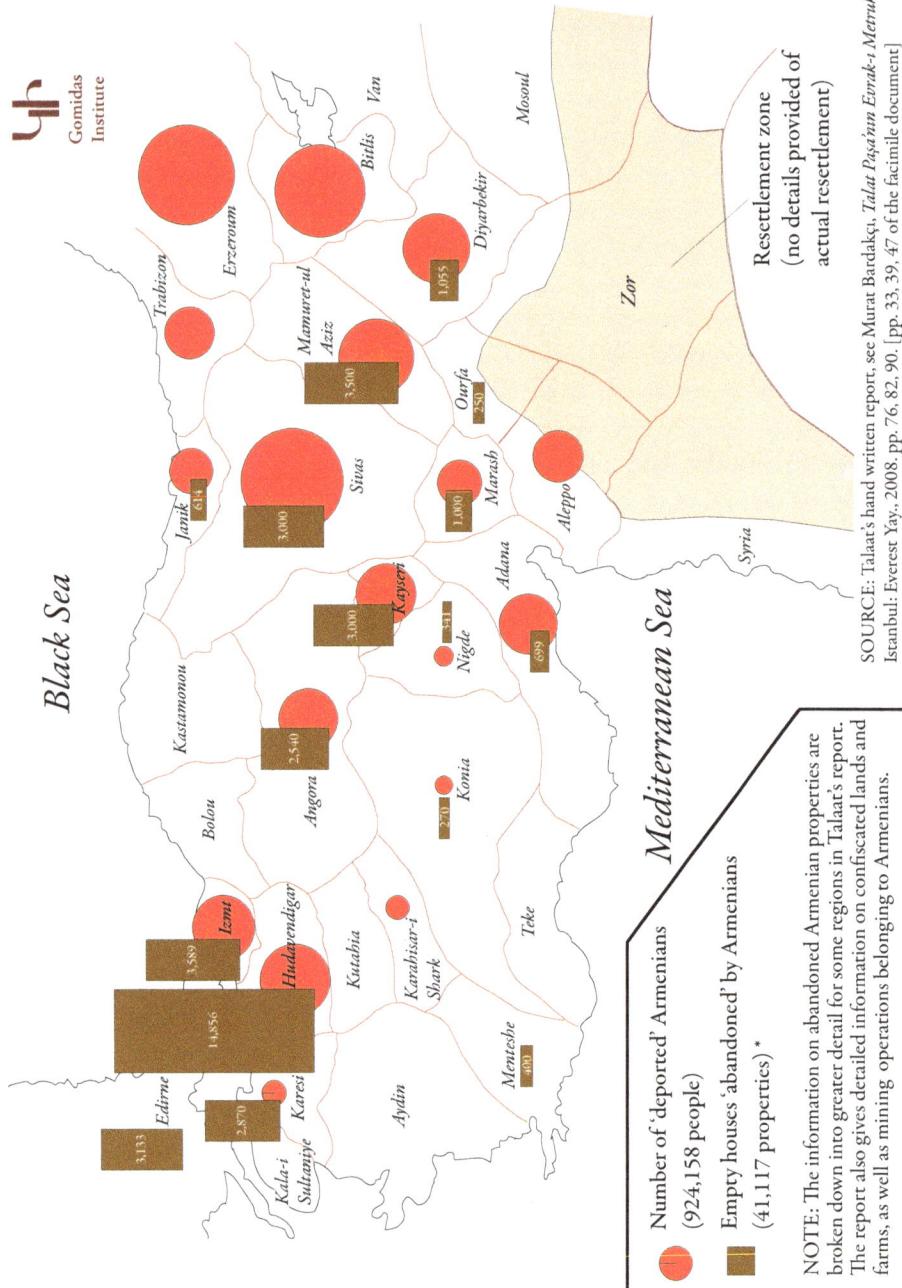

THE LIQUIDATION OF ARMENIANS AND
ARMENIAN PROPERTIES ACCORDING TO
TALAAT PASHA'S 'BLACK BOOK;'

APPENDED

Gomidas Institute

Black Sea

Mediterranean Sea

Trabizon
Erzeroum
Bitlis
Van
Diyarbekir
Mamuret-ul Aziz   1,055
Mosoul
3,500
Sivas
Janik   614
Ourfa   250
Marash
Zor
3,000
1,000
Kastamonou
Kayseri   Aleppo
3,000
Syria
Nigde   51
Adana
Angora   2,540   699
Bolou
Konia   270
Izmit   3,589
Hudavendigar
Kutahia
Teke
14,856   Karahisar-i Shark
Edirne   Menteshe   400
Kala-i Sultaniye   3,133   Aydin
Karesi   2,870

Resettlement zone
(no details provided of
actual resettlement)

SOURCE: Talaat's hand written report, see Murat Bardakçı, *Talat Paşa'nın Evrak-ı Metrukesi*,
Istanbul: Everest Yay., 2008. pp. 76, 82, 90. [pp. 33, 39, 47 of the facsimile document]

● Number of 'deported' Armenians
(924,158 people)

■ Empty houses 'abandoned' by Armenians
(41,117 properties) *

NOTE: The information on abandoned Armenian properties are
broken down into greater detail for some regions in Talaat's report.
The report also gives detailed information on confiscated lands and
farms, as well as mining operations belonging to Armenians.

Gomidas
Institute

Black Sea

Mediterranean Sea

Van

Bitlis

Mosul

Baghdad

Diyarbekir

Erzeroum   500
150

Trabizon
2,292

Mamuret-ul
Aziz
1,800

Zor
500

Syria

Ourfa

Janik   561
101

Sivas   70 ***
1,500

Marash   25
530 **

Aleppo
2,625

Kastamonou

Angora

Kaiseri

Nigde

Adana
415 *
90   55

Bolou

Izmit

Hudavendigar

Kutahia

Karahisar-i
Shark

Konia

Teke

Kala-i
Sultaniye

Karesi

Aydin

Menteshe

Constantinople

* Adana American Girls' College (400 girls) and
   Harouniye School (15 children).

** 530 children cared by two German women with Jemal
   Pasha's permission.

*** At Sivas Armenian orphanage.

Distributed within Muslim Community (6,743)

Remaining orphans (3,501)

Others 1,015

TOTAL 11,189 orphans

SOURCE: Talaat's hand written report, see Murat Bardakçı, *Talat Paşa'nın Evrak-ı Metrukesi*,
Istanbul: Everest Yay, 2008. p. 89 [p. 45 of the facsimile document]

**ARMENIAN ORPHANS RECORDED IN
TALAAT PASHA'S 'BLACK BOOK'**

The number of these "abandoned properties" does not correlate closely to the number of deported Armenians. For example, the number of houses in Sivas or Diyarbekir are too low given the number of Armenians who were deported from those provinces. There is no explanation accompanying these figures and the discrepancies may be explained in terms of the sequestration of such properties by local Muslim elites, individuals, and other officials during the genocidal process.[*]

A total of 90,458 donums of farmland is listed as abandoned by Armenians in another table entitled "Abandoned Armenian Farms." This list is also incomplete and only covers the vilayets of Ankara, Aleppo, and Sivas, the mutasarrifliks of Izmit, Urfa and Janik, and the [central] kazas of Marash and Afyon Karahisar, leaving out such major areas as Mamuretulaziz, Kayseri, Diyarbekir, and Adana.[†] The Armenian list is followed by another list of abandoned Greek properties in Edirne, Tekfurdagh (Rodosto), Kirkkilise and Gallipoli – indicating Talaat's hostile interest in the Greek population of the Ottoman Empire.

The booklet gives another list of confiscations in a table entitled "Land, Properties, Animals and Seed Given for the Settlement of [Muslim] Refugees in 1916." This list covers Ankara, Aydin, Istanbul, Aleppo, Hudavendigar, Mamuretulaziz, Izmit, Eskishehir, Janik, Marash, and Nigde, and records 20,545 houses, 267,536 donums of arable land, 76,942 donums of orchards, 7,812 donums of gardens, 703,491 donums of olive groves, 4,573 donums of mulberry trees, 97 donums of citrus (oranges), 5 carts, 4,390 animals, 2,912 agricultural implements, and 524,788 okes of seed.[‡] These properties were almost certainly taken from Ottoman Armenians and Greeks for the benefit of Muslim refugees and settlers covered in the first part of Talaat's black book.

Finally, the booklet presents a separate list of mines operated by Armenians in a table entitled "Mining Concessions Belonging to

---

[*] The number of people deported per abandoned home varied widely in these figures: Adana 66; Ankara 19; Janik 43; Diyarbekir 58; Hudavendigar 4.5; Izmit 15; Karesi 2.9; Kayseri 16; Konia 16; Mamuretulaziz 21; Nigde 15; Sivas 47. In most cases the number of abandoned Armenian properties registered with the state were too low.

[†] Bardakçı, pp. 100-101. The value of these farms was put at 3,852,551 kurush— excluding the 12,218 donums in Izmit which were not valued.

[‡] It is not clear if there was any overlap in this data with earlier figures, for example, for Armenian houses confiscated in the Mamuretulaziz region.

Armenians."[*] Presumably these concessions were simply taken over by state authorities.

Concluding Remarks

Talaat Pasha's personal, handwritten black book, replete with statistics, charts and color maps was almost certainly produced by Ottoman officials under instruction from Talaat Pasha, Minister of Interior and later Grand Vizier of the Ottoman Empire. Talaat even took this book into exile with him, when he fled the Ottoman Empire in 1918. Undoubtedly, given the incriminating content, Talaat would certainly have destroyed this book, along with his actual report on the Armenian Genocide, were it not for his untimely death in Berlin, at the age of 46, in 1921. The fortuitous survival of these materials, first with Talaat's widow and then Murat Bardakçı, a family friend, who published them in facsimile format has allowed us fascinating glimpses into Talaat Pasha's inner world.

The format and choice of topics constituting the black book reflect Talaat's abiding interest in the social engineering of the Ottoman Empire through the mass settlement of Muslim emigrants and refugees in Ottoman domains and the systematic liquidation of non-Muslim communities, most notably Armenians.

The genocide of Armenians, as covered in the black book, is with reference to three pillars of the genocidal process Talaat oversaw: the systematic destruction of Armenian communities through mass-deportation and murder; the mass-absorption of Armenian women and children into Muslim households; and the mass-expropriation of Armenian properties. The black book couches these processes in softer but clear terms, such as the "transfer" of Armenians communities instead of deportations and killings, "taking care" of Armenian orphans in Muslim communities, and managing properties "abandoned" by their rightful, Armenian owners. Talaat's report on the Armenian Genocide in the first part of this study, on the other hand, is more explicit and relates the fact that the number of Armenian deportees in 1915 was much higher than the official figures indicated in the black book, and that most deportees actually disappeared during the deportation process or in the Der Zor and surrounding "resettlement area" – facts attested to by survivors of massacres and other onlookers.

---

[*] Bardakçı, pp. 102-103.

Gomidas Institute Publications

Child Victims of the Armenian Genocide.

www.gomidas.org

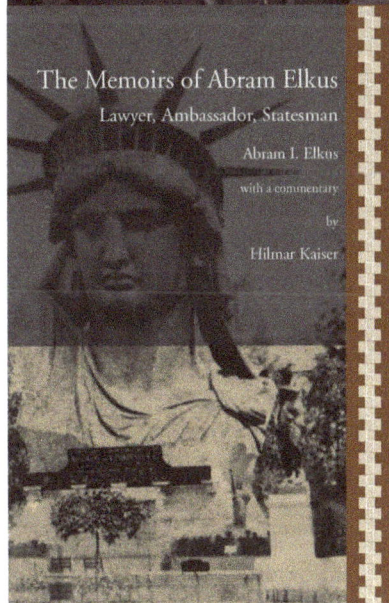

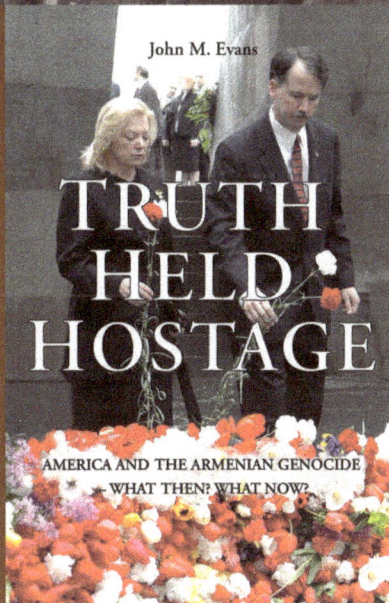

NEW EDITION

UNITED STATES OFFICIAL RECORDS ON THE ARMENIAN GENOCIDE, 1915-17

Compiled and edited by Ara Sarafian

James Bryce and Arnold Toynbee

The Treatment of Armenians in the Ottoman Empire 1915-1916

Documents Presented to Viscount Grey of Fallodon by Viscount Bryce

Uncensored Edition

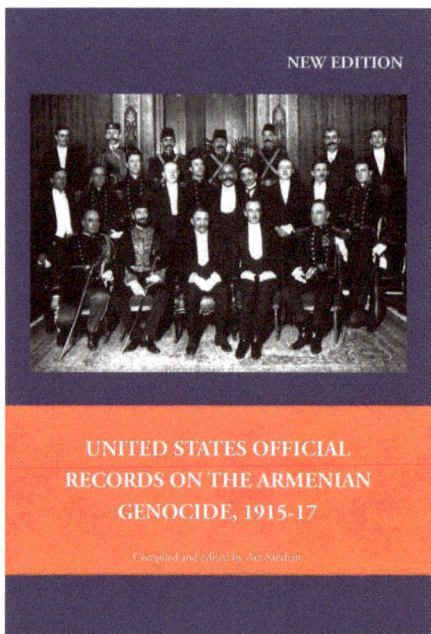

Two seminal works on the Armenian Genocide.

A systematic collection of United States consular and diplomatic reports on the Armenian Genocide, *United States Official Records on the Armenian Genocide, 1915-17.* These are among the core records that informed Henry Morgenthau, the American ambassador in Constantinople, and the United States government in Washington DC about the mass extermination of Ottoman Armenians in 1915.

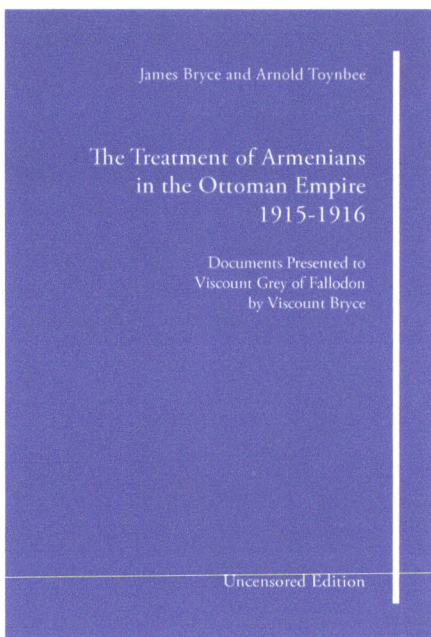

The critical "uncensored edition" of the 1916 British Parliamentary Blue Book, *The Treatment of Armenians in the Ottoman Empire, 1915-1916,* was the first systematic thesis of the Armenian Genocide. It was published in 1916 and was largely based on United States consular records from the Ottoman Empire. This annotated edition is a seminal work in its own right.

Both titles have been published by the Gomidas Institute.

www.gomidas.org

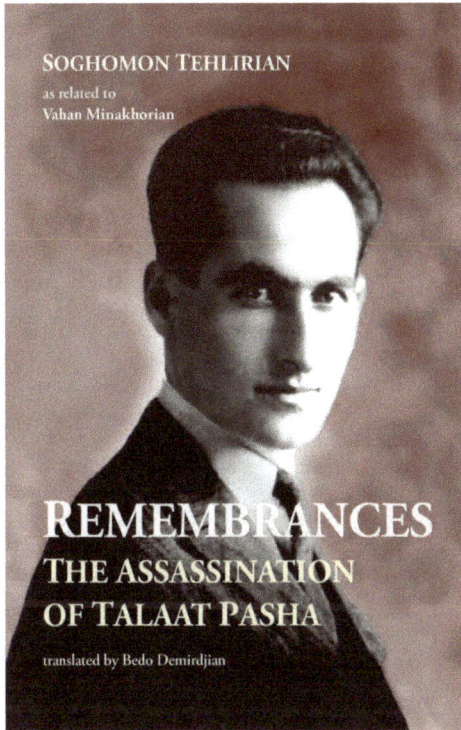

Soghomon Tehlirian, *Remembrances: The Assassination of Talaat Pasha*, as told to Vahan Minakhorian and translated from Armenian by Bedo Demirdjian, (London: Gomidas Institute, 2022), ISBN 978-1-909382-54-1. An epic story of gigantic proportions, this is an account of one of the great assassinations of the 20th century, the killing of Talaat Pasha, the architect of the Armenian Genocide of 1915. The assassination took place in Berlin on 15 March 1921. Tehlirian was subsequently tried and found not guilty.

www.gomidas.org

** Կիր**

Gomidas Institute
42 Blythe Rd.
London W14 0HA
England

Email: *info@gomidas.org*
Web: *www.gomidas.org*

www.ingramcontent.com/pod-product-compliance
Lightning Source LLC
Chambersburg PA
CBHW040136270326
41927CB00019B/3405